D1447358

CHRISTIAN BELIEFS AND TEACHINGS

Second Edition

John C. Meyer

University Press of America, Inc.
Lanham • New York • Oxford

Copyright © 1997 by
University Press of America,® Inc.
4720 Boston Way
Lanham, Maryland 20706

12 Hid's Copse Rd.
Cummor Hill, Oxford OX2 9JJ

Library of Congress Cataloging-in-Publication Data

Meyer, John C.
Christian beliefs and teachings / John C. Meyer, --2nd ed.
p.   cm.
Includes bibliographical references and Index.
l. Theology, Doctrinal--Popular works. I. Title.
BT77.M48   1997   230--dc21   97-20085 CIP

ISBN 0-7618-0802-7 (cloth: alk. ppr.)
ISBN 0-7618-0803-5 (pbk: alk. ppr.)

TABLE OF CONTENTS

Preface

It has been sixteen years since this book was first published. As was pointed out in the first edition of this book, a substantial need on the part of the author for a textbook to use in the college classroom was the impetus for writing this volume. Since the fall of 1969, the author has been teaching a college level course in the field of Christian theology at an independent, non-sectarian university. His failure to find an adequate textbook to use in class initially led to the writing of this book. This same need still exists today. All too often textbooks in the field of Religious Studies have been written from a particular denominational point of view or from a disparaging, non-sympathetic view toward the Christian religion. Attempting to overcome this lacuna the author, at the encouragement of his students, had published the original version in 1981. Recently he was again encouraged to update and revise the original book.

The revised edition contains new material taking into consideration theological developments in recent years. It also has the addition of a glossary and an index which the first edition lacked. Some of the material is presented in a different way with the hope that it will become more clear to the reader.

Again, it has been the intention of the author to present this primer of the traditional basic beliefs of Christians while trying to avoid any form of denominational bias. This book is, therefore, primarily intended not to take sides while presenting the major interpretations found among Christians with regard to their fundamental beliefs. Nor does the author ridicule or play down any recognized point of view. However, the author is also well aware that no human person is without his or her biases or preconceptions.

The method that is usually followed by the author in the explanation of these traditional Christian beliefs begins with looking at some of the biblical material behind the beliefs found in both the Old Testament and the New

Testament. After the biblical basis for the beliefs is explained an attempt is made to show how a particular belief developed in the history of the Christian religion. Finally, the contemporary understanding of those beliefs is dealt with while trying to show the religious pluralism found within Christianity, the world's most numerous religion.

The author is indebted to all of his students throughout the years who have studied with him in this endeavor. He is also grateful to his wife, Mary Claire, and his son, John David, for their loving encouragement and forbearance. *Mulieris fortis et filii benigni beatus vir.*

jcm

Acknowledgment

Scripture quotations are from the Revised Standard Version of the Bible, copyright 1946, 1952, 1971 by the Division of Christian Education of the National Council of the Churches of Christ in the USA. Used by permission.

Chapter 1

The Christian God

It seems that a good starting place for any textbook on religion purporting to explain the basic Christian beliefs is with its attempt to investigate the concept of Ultimate Reality itself. Traditionally, Christians have referred to Ultimate Reality, the supreme power in the universe and the source of all that exists, by the term, God. This chapter will study the Christian concept of God especially as belief in this Ultimate Reality unfolds in the pages of the Christian scriptures, the Bible. Various Christian views of God and God's relation to the universe also will be examined.

A. The Biblical Concept of God

1. *The Old Testament.* The first part of the Christian Bible comprises essentially the Jewish scriptures. It deals with a people's coming to believe in only one God among all the gods that many neighboring peoples admitted to exist. Strictly speaking, the descendants of Abraham, the Israelites, had no doctrine concerning their belief in God. There was no speculation about God. Nevertheless, there was no question about God's existence. God was quite simply experienced by the Israelites.

From about the time of Abraham, who is generally dated from about the twentieth century B.C., until about the sixth century B.C., there was a problem among the Israelites regarding their belief in God as they evolved from polytheism through henotheism to strict monotheism. Whereas polytheism is defined as a belief in many gods, henotheism worships a single god without denying the existence of other inferior gods as well. Monotheism explicitly affirms the existence of and worships only one deity alone. Throughout much of the history of the Israelite people recounted in the pages of the Old Testament, the people are continually being tempted by the polytheistic beliefs of their neighbors. What is more, their ancestors themselves were undoubtedly polytheistic as well. However, at least from about the time of the Babylonian Exile in the sixth century B.C., the Israelites had indeed evolved to a strict monotheistic belief reflected in the central prayer of the Jewish religion, the *Shema Israel*: "Hear, O Israel: the Lord our God is one Lord; and you shall love the Lord your God with all your heart, and with all your soul, and with all your might" (Dt. 6:4-5). It is this strict belief in one God alone that Jesus identifies with in the New Testament. He described God as "the God of Abraham, and the God of Isaac, and the God of Jacob" (Mt. 22:32) referring to the patriarchs of the Israelites and their belief in the same God. As a matter of fact, in the New Testament when Jesus was questioned about the greatest commandment of the Law, he answered by quoting from the *Shema Israel*: "Hear, O Israel: The Lord our God, the Lord is one; and you shall love the Lord your God with all your heart, and with all your soul, and with all your mind, and with all your strength" (Mk. 12:29-30).

The various names that the Old Testament employs for God also indicate how the Israelites came to view their God. The proper name for God that appears thousands of times in the pages of the Old Testament consists of four Hebrew consonants, *YHWH*.[1] This is the name that God himself made known to the Israelites through his prophet, Moses, and it is never used to refer to the false, pagan deities. After God appeared to Moses in the burning bush and had commissioned him to return to Egypt to lead the Israelites out of their servitude and towards the Promised Land, Moses asked God his name to tell the people. God responded to Moses' question by referring to himself as *YHWH*, usually pronounced as Yahweh and translated as "I am who I am," a form of the verb "to be." Scholars generally interpret this proper name of God to mean that the Judaeo-Christian God is one who exists and who will always exist without depending upon any other being for existence. The pertinent biblical text reads as follows:

> Then Moses said to God, "If I come to the people of Israel and say to them 'The God of your fathers has sent me to you,' and they ask me, 'What is his name?' what shall I say to them?" God said to Moses, "I AM WHO I AM." And he said, "Say this to the people of Israel, 'I AM has sent me to you.'" (Ex. 3:13-14)

The Israelites developed such great reverence for this proper name of God that after the year 70 A.D. they did not even dare to pronounce this sacred name, but believers substituted other Hebrew words in place of their God's name. This old attitude of not being willing to attempt to control God by pronouncing the name of God is reflected among present day Jews as well who generally write God's name G_d. Traditionally, among the Israelites, to name something is to be in control of that which is named, as God is in control of the universe.

Common names for God found in the pages of the Old Testament also tell us much about the Israelite understanding of God. The names *El, Eloah,* and *Elohim* are popular names among all ancient Semitic peoples to indicate divinity. These names indicating divinity are generally attached to other Hebrew words indicating how the Israelites viewed their God. Some of these expressions found in the Old Testament are El *Shaddai*[2] meaning God almighty; *El Elyon*[3] indicating God most high, teaching the transcendence of their God; and *El Olam*[4] meaning the everlasting God. Another Hebrew term that is often used for God in the pages of the Old Testament is the word *Adonai*[5] meaning lords or one who has authority. *Adonai is* generally used for the sacred letters *YHWH* in the Hebrew Bible. *Jehovah,* which first appeared in Christian versions of the Old Testament in the late thirteenth century A.D., is a corruption of the vowels from *Adonai* and the consonants *YHWH* made by a translator.[6] The name Jehovah itself is meaningless in Hebrew, but taken as a combination of the tetragrammaton, *YHWH*, and the title, *Adonai,* it has great meaning for many Christians.

Throughout the pages of the Old Testament God is presented as a real person and at times is spoken of in an anthropomorphic manner, that is, as if God were in the form of a human. However, especially after the time of the Babylonian Exile in the sixth century B.C., God is presented more as a spiritual and transcendent God in the pages of the Old Testament.

Of all God's attributes gleaned from a reading of the Old Testament, it appears that his holiness or sanctity is primary.[7] God's holiness is emphasized frequently in the pages of the Old Testament. God is indeed also the all powerful[8] God who not only creates from nothing, but also sustains all creation in its existence. God is a sublime[9] God, one who is most high and elevated over all creation. God is an eternal[10] God who never had a beginning and who will never have an end. The immutability[11] of God is also described in the Old Testament literature insofar as God is an unchanging God. His ubiquity[12] or omnipresence is also taught. Moreover, God is not only found among the Chosen People, but also among the other nations as well. The God of the Old Testament is a very wise[13] and omniscient [14] God. God's wisdom is unsurpassable among people and God's knowledge, even of hidden things, is well known.

But in God's relationship to human beings, God is continually presented as a good[15] and merciful[16] God, one who is always truthful[17]   and faithful.[18]   God is invariably faithful to any bargain, agreement, or covenant; human beings are pictured as violating these contracts and pacts with God and thereby sinning. But the God of the Old Testament is also a just[19] God. God's goodness and mercy are balanced by God's justice, and when the Israelites stray from the path of righteousness in their relationship with God, they are quickly brought to repentance by God's just punishment. Nevertheless, God's abiding love for creation and especially for human beings is witnessed to in the books of the Old Testament. God's love is compared to conjugal love between a husband and his wife in the prophetic writings[20] of the Old Testament; elsewhere it is seen as a paternal love, the love that a father has for his children.[21] Rarely is this love seen as love for an individual person, but more often it is seen as God's love for the people in general.

2. *The New Testament.* Whereas in the Old Testament there was one God and one person of God depicted in God's relationship with the Israelites, the New Testament concept of God adds the notion that although there is but one God, there are three different aspects or persons in God. For example, when Jesus gives his followers the charge to preach the gospel he says: "Go therefore and make disciples of all nations, baptizing them in the name of the Father and of the Son and of the Holy Spirit" (Mt. 28:19). The radical monotheism of the Old Testament is accepted by the writers of the New Testament, but there is also the affirmation of what Christians refer to as the Trinity of persons in God, a belief proper to the Christian religion.

The first person of the Trinity is God the Father. This aspect of God was basically revealed during Old Testament times and the God of the Old Testament is generally looked upon as God the Father. Whereas the Son and the Holy Spirit can also be found as being referred to in the pages of the Old Testament, many Christian theologians prefer to see God the Father as essentially being referred to in the books of the Old Testament. As a matter of fact, to this day religious Jews admit only one person in the one God. However, the Christian scriptures include both the Old and the New Testaments and their belief about God is based upon both of these major components of their Bible.

The Son of God is the second person of the Trinity of persons in God. Based upon the New Testament primarily, Christians believe that Jesus, whom they affirm as the Christ or Messiah, is both the Son of God and the Son of Man. Christian Christology teaches that Jesus is both fully divine and fully human. As Son of God his sanctity was emphasized at his baptism in the Jordan River at the beginning of his public life.

> In those days Jesus came from Nazareth of Galilee and was baptized by John in the Jordan. And when he came up out of the water, immediately he saw the heavens opened and the Spirit descending upon him like a dove; and a voice came from heaven, "Thou art my beloved Son; with thee I am well pleased." (Mk. 1:9-11)

Possessing the divine prerogative, Jesus, as the Son of God, goes about performing miracles, forgiving sins, and teaching with the authority of God.

At the same time, however, Jesus is also the Son of Man. According to the New Testament and the Christian belief in the Incarnation, Jesus was conceived and born of a woman, and lived a truly human existence insofar as he nourished his body, gave way to human emotion, suffered, and even died. Perhaps St. Paul's Letter to the Philippians in the New Testament best sums up this union of the humanity and the divinity in the one person of Jesus:

> Have this mind among yourselves, which you have in Christ Jesus, who, though he was in the form of God, did not count equality with God a thing to be grasped, but emptied himself, taking the form of a servant, being born in the likeness of men. (Phil. 2:5-7)

The study of Jesus with regard to both his divinity and his humanity is referred to by Christians as Christology.

The third person in God is the Holy Spirit. At the conception of Jesus the Holy Spirit is mentioned as being instrumental in joining the humanity to the divinity of Jesus. "And the angel said to her [Mary], 'The Holy Spirit will come upon you, and the power of the Most High will overshadow you; therefore the child to be born will be called holy, the Son of God'" (Lk. 1:35). The Book of the Acts of the Apostles in the New Testament tells the story of the descent of the Holy Spirit upon the followers of Jesus after Jesus' death and resurrection.

> When the day of Pentecost had come, they were all together in one place. And suddenly a sound came from heaven like the rush of a mighty wind, and it filled all the house where they were sitting. And there appeared to them tongues as of fire, distributed and resting on each one of them. And they were all filled with the Holy Spirit and began to speak in other tongues, as the Spirit gave them utterance. (Acts 2:1-4)

Especially does St. Paul in the New Testament emphasize the gifts of the Holy Spirit that the followers of Jesus possess.[22] Those Christians who particularly highlight the action of the Holy Spirit in their lives are generally referred to as Pentecostal or Charismatic Christians. They continue to believe in and practice such phenomena as glossolalia or the speaking in tongues, spiritual healing, prophecy, the interpretation of tongues, etc. The study of the Holy Spirit among Christians is technically classified as pneumatology.

B. Traditional Doctrine of the Trinity

Whereas the Christian doctrine of the Trinity is in the realm of faith for Christians and is essentially one of the great mysteries of the Christian faith, from earliest times Christian creeds have affirmed this belief. For example, the Apostles' Creed, in its earliest form that developed at Rome about the end of the second century A.D. professed belief in the trinity of persons in God. The present form of the Apostles' Creed dates from about 700 A.D. and follows the same earliest Trinitarian theological formulas.[23] The Christian doctrine of the Trinity tries to elucidate the picture of God as he appears in the Bible and in the history of the Christian community. Therefore, traditionally Christians have taught that their understanding of God includes one divine nature and three distinct persons.

Based upon the definition principally of the Council of Nicea in 325 A.D., the unity of God is expressed in one "substance" or "essence". These words are English translations for the Greek word *ousia* and the Latin word *substantia*. The Christian Council of Nicea, called by the Roman emperor, Constantine, to deal with disputed matters in the Christian Church in the fourth century, defined that the Father and the Son are of the same nature or substance. This definition, in effect, condemned what since has been known as the heresy of Arianism that taught that Jesus was only a created being. At the Council of Constantinople in 381 A.D. it was also declared by the leaders of the Christian Church that the Holy Spirit is of the same nature as both the

Father and the Son. Therefore, from earliest times, the Christian Church has taught that each of the persons of the Trinity is God, that all three persons are equal with regard to perfection and attributes. However, there is but one God and one divine nature.

It was also declared at the Council of Nicea, whence Christians received the famous Nicene Creed, that there are three persons in God. The Greek term they used at Nicea was *hypostasis* meaning literally "standing under." This was translated into the Latin *persona* from which we get the English word person. The Christian Church has never defined what it meant by *hypostasis*, but simply used the term to show distinction among the three. Some Christian thinkers prefer to think of three movements or modes of being in God. Nonetheless, it must be remembered that there are not three beings in God, but only one being that the theologian Paul Tillich was fond of referring to as "the Ground of Being," that God does not merely exist, he is the very source of all beings that exist and existence itself.[24]

C. A Contemporary Understanding of the Trinity

The distinguished Christian theologian, John Macquarrie, in his book titled *Principles of Christian Theology* gives an existential-ontological statement of the meaning of the Trinity in contemporary language. He begins by affirming that God can best be understood in the language of being since indeed the proper name for God, made known to Moses on Mt. Sinai, has the verb "to be" at its root. The name, *YHWH*,[25] is generally translated to mean "I am who I am," as was indicated earlier. Macquarrie sees Jesus identifying with this proper name for God in the New Testament with the statement: "Before Abraham was, I am" (Jn. 8:58). By this, Jesus is indicating that he is one with the Father. As Macquarrie states:

> It can hardly be doubted that the "I am" here is an allusion to the "I am" of the Old Testament. In any case, the saying is meant to assert the intimate relationship of Christ to the Father, and it expresses this in terms of being. Here then we see the doctrine of God as Being converging with the emerging doctrine of God as Trinity, for it is being ("I am") which expresses the unity of the first two persons of the Trinity.[26]

In other words, according to Macquarrie, God can be understood as Being which has let itself be known under the trinitarian symbolism of Father, Son, and Holy Spirit.

This Being is both a dynamic and stable mystery. The Father can be referred to as "primordial Being"[27] insofar as the Father is that person in God who brings other beings into existence or lets beings be, to use a Tillichian phrase. The Son may be called "expressive Being"[28] because the Son is the Word of God as he is referred to especially in the Gospel according to John. It is the Son then who expresses the Being of God in all other beings. To quote Macquarrie again:

> The primordial Being of the Father, which would otherwise be entirely hidden, flows out through expressive Being to find its expression in the world of beings. Christians believe that the Father's Being finds expression above all in the finite being of Jesus, and in such a way that his being is caught up into Being itself.[29]

Traditionally, Christians have looked upon Jesus as the sum total of God's revelation to human beings in line with the Epistle to the Hebrews' statement: "In many and various ways God spoke of old to our fathers by the prophets; but in these last days he has spoken to us by a Son, whom he appointed the heir of all things, through whom also he created the world" (Heb. 1:1-2). The Holy Spirit can be named "unitive Being".[30] It is the Holy Spirit who relates and unites beings to Being itself. Therefore, to understand the activity of the Holy Spirit would constantly view this person of the Trinity as maintaining, strengthening, and restoring the unity of Being with beings.[31] It must be remembered that Macquarrie is not affirming three beings in God, rather he is positing one Being and then explaining three aspects of this one Being, especially as this Being is related to all other beings. But the mystery remains. Many catechists have attempted to use analogies such as the shamrock with its three leaves and one stem, the figure of a triangle with its three sides, or three-in-one oil with its special blend of oils. But all analogies limp and are inadequate. Nevertheless, because Christians believe in a personal God who is directly related to them in their everyday lives, they are continually attempting to shed some light especially on the major mysteries of their faith. Furthermore, some feminist theologians prefer to speak of the three distinctions in God in the gender neutral terms of Creator, Liberator and Sustainer. Yet in the end, faith is just that. It is always beyond reason.

D. The Attributes of God

The question is asked whether or not finite human beings can even begin to fathom what God is like. It is realized that one cannot analyze God in the same way that one can dissect and inspect human beings and the world they live in. Everything that is asserted about God should be first based upon God's own revelation to people throughout the ages. God always remains a mystery and whatever one asserts about God, based on God's own revelation, needs in some way to be qualified too because God is always much more than that described by human, finite language.[32] Some have maintained that the best way to speak about God is either by using negative language,[33] thereby leaving the issue about God's perfections open, or by silently acknowledging the very presence of God experientially.[34] Others have attempted to explain all about God and have ended up by taking the mystery out of the Christian religion itself.[35] One wonders what is left of religion after all has been explained away and no faith commitment is any longer required.

Possibly the better way to speak about the attributes of God is by acknowledging the mysterious nature of the Christian God as being primary. This mysterious God has revealed himself in a threefold manner of Father, Son, and Holy Spirit. Beyond that, one can only deal with limited comparisons. Whereas God's creation is finite and dependent upon God for its existence, God is infinite and in every way independent of and beyond creation. Therefore, Christians do indeed speak of their God as omnipotent, omniscient, ubiquitous, immeasurable, incomprehensible, all good, eternal, immutable, holy, sinless, all just, all merciful, all loving, and so on. Not only are they basing their beliefs here upon their reading of the Bible, but they are also continually comparing the mysterious God with themselves and their world which they deem to be limited and imperfect. All of God's attributes are fragmentary and complement one another. There is no final and complete description of God in human, finite language.

Perhaps there is no perfection of God that expresses the reality of the Christian God better than the one defining God as love. This definition of God is found in the New Testament: "Beloved, let us love one another; for love is of God, and he who loves is born of God and knows God. He who does not love does not know God; for God is love" (1 Jn. 4:7-8). It would seem that the biblical writer here is teaching that the best way to come to know the Christian God is by loving, because the self-giving love of God is the point of closest contact that humans have with the sublime God. There are always two realities, God and humans, in relationship with one another. They never become identical or fused. Because God is holy, God will always remain wholly other than creation, but

Christians believe that it is possible for sinful people to draw close to God in an intimate, loving relationship.[36] How people are enabled to do this will be the topic of scrutiny in a later chapter.

E. Divine Revelation

Throughout this present chapter references have been made to the Christian belief that God not only exists but has made himself known to human beings. The Christian doctrine of revelation attempts to describe the various ways God has communicated information about himself to people. In fact, the word "reveal" means to make known, to make unhidden, to uncover or to remove the veil. Therefore, the basic content of revelation is the person of God becoming known to humans throughout the years. One Christian theologian defines revelation as "...a personal union in knowledge between God and a participating subject in the revelational history of a community."[37] Basically, the purpose of divine revelation is to help a person answer the question of the meaning of life as a whole; such fundamental questions as where did I come from, where am I going and what should I be doing in the meantime.

Christian theology generally recognizes two distinct types of revelation: natural, general, or universal revelation and supernatural, special, or particular revelation. The first type of revelation is believed to be present in the natural order of history and generally or universally present in the actions of human beings. This means that God makes himself known to people through a variety of natural means, as he is present everywhere in the world. The three major ways God is present to all people, even non-Christians, consist of all human beings reflecting the image of God, God being the creator and sustainer of life, and the belief that God is behind the moral order within history.

The very first book of the Bible teaches that human beings were created by God to God's own image and likeness.[38] Christians thus believe that there is a certain co-naturality between human beings and God. A human person is like God, but yet is not God. Nevertheless, a person continually seeks the reality that produces the image itself. Insofar as God created people to his own image, God is present to each person and thus has revealed something of himself by using himself in some way as a pattern for creating human beings.

But not only did God create human beings, he created all beings that exist outside himself and he sustains those created beings in their existence. God consequently gives purpose, order, and design to all of creation. He is behind the cycle of the seasons, the death of vegetation and its renewal again, the succession of one generation following another in the pattern of birth, growth, death, and decay. Therefore, by creating and sustaining life, God has made himself known to the entire human race.

Thirdly, general revelation is also the notion that there is a moral order behind history itself. It is God who guarantees this order, insofar as, generally speaking, evil deeds get punished naturally and good deeds are naturally rewarded. It is this fundamental belief among many people that has led to the hackneyed aphorism: "Virtue is its own reward." Again, this type of natural, general or universal revelation is open to all human beings, and if people try hard enough, perhaps they can discover this presence of God in the world about them.

The other major type of divine revelation is called supernatural, special, or particular revelation because it has taken place at a definite time and place in history. This type of revelation comprises the belief that God has manifested himself to people through certain events and persons, especially through the person of Jesus Christ.

While reading particularly the pages of the Old Testament, it is noticed that God is explicitly acting in certain events described there. For example, God is seen as leading the Israelites out of their Egyptian captivity during the time of the Exodus; God is depicted as being with his people while they are conquering the Promised Land; and God is also described as punishing his people for their unfaithfulness to their covenantal relationship with him. While acting in these events, Christians believe that God is revealing himself to people in a special way, beyond the ordinary.

Moreover, the books of the Old Testament teach that God singled out certain individuals to be his intermediaries while dealing with his people. These agents of God are called prophets. He not only made himself known through these individuals, but he also revealed his will for his people through them. However, there was one person who comprised the fulness of God's revelation to humans, Jesus Christ, the God-Man. Because Jesus Christ is believed by Christians to be truly God, he is the sum total of God's revelation to human beings. Christians assert then that God revealed himself fully and completely in the person of Jesus.[39]

Even though God has totally revealed himself to the human race in the person of Jesus Christ, people have not been able to grasp completely this reality because of their finitude and God's infinity. However, Jesus is believed to be still alive in his church, and so revelation continues as

Christians encounter him as individuals in the Christian community. As Jesus Christ becomes better known through the guidance and inspiration of the Holy Spirit, so too then does revelation continue in the Christian community. The eminent Christian theologian, Karl Rahner, used the analogy here of people in love growing in that love as time progresses.[40] They were in love all the while, but their love for one another continues to grow and expand bringing about new dimensions of knowledge of one another in the loving relationship. Because of this continuing revelation in the Christian community, Christian creeds have grown and have become modified too throughout the years. In other words, because of the belief in continuing revelation there is also the corresponding belief in doctrinal development. The active principle here again is the Holy Spirit whose power "blows where it wills" (Jn. 3:8). As Jesus indicated, the Holy Spirit "will guide you into all the truth; for he will speak, and he will declare to you the things that are to come" (Jn. 16:13).

Notes - Chapter 1

1.The original Hebrew scriptures were written in consonantal form. Much later, however, vowels were added to the consonants to indicate how the Hebrew words were to be accurately pronounced. The Hebrew text with both the consonants and the vowels is generally referred to as the Masoretic Text named after the scribal interpreters called Masoretes who accomplished this task.

2.E.g., Ex. 6:2-3.

3.E.g., Gen. 14:18-20.

4.E.g., Gen. 21:33.

5.E.g., Gen. 24:12.

6.Cf. Bernhard W. Anderson, *Understanding the Old Testament* (Englewood Cliffs, N.J.: Prentice-Hall, Inc., 1963), 34.

7.E.g., Num. 20:12-13 and Is. 6:3.

8.E.g., Ex. 15:1-3.

9.E.g., Ps. 11:4.

10.E.g., Ps. 90:1-4.

11.E.g., Ps. 102:26-28.

12.E.g., Ps. 139:7-10.

13.E.g., Is. 55:8-9.

14.E.g., Ps. 139:1-6.

15.E.g., Ps. 31:19.

16.E.g., Ps. 103:8-14.

17.E.g., Ps. 25:5.

18.E.g., Ps. 91:4.

19.E.g., Is. 11:3-5.

20.E.g., Hos. 2:14-20.

21.E.g., Ex. 4:22-23.

22.Cf. 1 Cor. 12:4-11 and Gal. 5:16-25.

23.Cf. John H. Leith, *Creeds of the Churches* (Chicago: Aldine Publishing Co., 1963), 22-25. The text of the Apostles' Creed is found on pp. 24-25 as follows: "I believe in God the Father almighty, creator of heaven and earth; And in Jesus Christ, His only Son, our Lord, Who was conceived by the Holy Spirit, born of the Virgin Mary, suffered under Pontius Pilate, was crucified, dead and buried. He descended to hell, on the third day rose again from the dead, ascended to heaven, sits at the right hand of God the Father almighty, thence He will come to judge the living and the dead; I believe in the Holy Spirit, the holy catholic Church, the communion of saints, the forgiveness of sins, the resurrection of the body [carnis], and life everlasting. Amen."

24. "However it is defined, the 'existence of God' contradicts the idea of a creative ground of essence and existence. The ground of being cannot be found within the totality of beings, nor can the ground of essence and existence participate in the tensions and disruptions characteristic of the transition from essence to existence...God does not exist. He is being-itself beyond essence and existence. Therefore, to argue that God exists is to deny him." Paul Tillich, *Systematic Theology*, I (N.Y.: Harper and Row, 1967), 204-205.

25.Cf. Ex. 3:14.

26.John Macquarrie, *Principles of Christian Theology*, second edition (N.Y.: Chas. Scribner's Sons, 1977), 197.

27.Ibid., 198.

28.Ibid., 199.

29.Ibid., 199-200.

30.Cf. Macquarrie, *op. cit.*, 201.

31.Ibid.

32.Cf. John Macquarrie, *God-Talk* (N.Y.: Harper and Row, 1967), 228 ff. where he speaks of the paradoxical character of symbolic language.

33.Cf. Dietrich Bonhoeffer, *Christ the Center* (N.Y.: Harper and Row, 1966), 91-93, 101, 105-106. Bonhoeffer claims that the greatness of the Council of Chalcedon (451) lay in the fact that it described Jesus Christ in negative terminology, thus leaving much room for doctrinal development in Christology.

34.Cf. Abraham Joshua Heschel, *Between God and Man*, edited by Fritz A. Rothschild (N.Y.: The Free Press, 1959), 72-79, where Heschel asserts that the ineffable God is revealed to people in the form of hiddenness and requires a special sensitivity by them to become aware of God.

35.This has been one of the major criticisms of some liberal Christian theology in contemporary times.

36.Cf. Rudolf Otto, *Idea of the Holy*, second edition (N.Y.: Oxford University Press, 1950).

37.Gabriel Moran, *Theology of Revelation* (N.Y.: Herder and Herder, 1966), 93.

38.Cf. Gen. 1:26-27.

39.Cf. Heb. 1:1-2.

40.Cf. Karl Rahner, "The Development of Dogma," *Theological Investigations*, I (Baltimore: Helicon Press, 1961), 63-65.

Chapter 2

Jesus Christ

Without a doubt, Jesus Christ is the center of focus for Christians throughout the ages. However, outside the Christian Church, Jesus has, at times, been looked upon as merely a great teacher or prophet. This, for example, would be the Jewish or Muslim view of Jesus. It sees him as entirely human and not divine; he is not a savior, but a mere man. Other non-Christians have a relativistic view of Jesus, insofar as they see him simply as another good man in history. This comprises the modern, secular view of Jesus. Still others look at Jesus as the perfect man, the ideal man to be imitated by others, but not divine. This is the humanist-perfectionist view of Jesus held by certain secular humanists and even by some very liberal Christian groups. There is, however, the more orthodox or classical Christian view of Jesus that sees him as both fully human and fully divine, the God-Man. This is the view of Jesus with which this chapter will be concerned. Central to this view is the Christian doctrine of the Incarnation of Jesus which teaches that the Son of God, the second person of the Trinity of persons in God, took on human flesh and became man. He is both, therefore, Son of God and truly human too.

A. Son of God

The traditional Christian doctrine referring to the union of the two natures (human and divine) in the one person of Jesus Christ has been called the doctrine of the hypostatic union, from the Greek word, *hypostasis*, meaning person or individual being. This word was taken from the usage of it made by the Council of Nicea in 325 A.D. while defining that the Son of God is consubstantial to the Father, as was explained in the preceding chapter. Whereas the Council of Nicea was combating the major heresy of Arianism,[1] in the following century two other Christological heresies had arrived on the scene. It was a time of clarification. One of these beliefs was referred to as Nestorianism,[2] which claimed that there are two persons in Jesus Christ, a divine person and a human person. The other heresy, Monophysitism,[3] taught that there was only one nature in Jesus Christ and that nature was divine. Therefore, another ecumenical or general council was called within the Christian Church to decide these issues. It took place at Chalcedon in 451 A.D. The Christological definition of Chalcedon stated that Jesus Christ "...is perfect both in deity and also in humanness...is also actually God and actually man...in two natures...in one person and in one *hypostasis*...."[4] Therefore, at Chalcedon, Nestorianism and Monophysitism stood condemned as heresies by the more orthodox Christian church. There are two distinct natures in Jesus Christ not confused nor divided, but united in one person. Jesus Christ is believed by Christians in general then to be truly God and truly man.

Perhaps the most balanced statement of both aspects of Jesus Christ is found again in St. Paul's New Testament letter to the Philippians:

> Have this mind among yourselves, which you have in Christ Jesus, who, though he was in the form of God, did not count equality with God a thing to be grasped, but emptied himself, taking the form of a servant, being born in the likeness of men (Phil. 2:5-7).[5]

Insofar as Jesus Christ is both truly God and truly man, he is not a mere intermediary between God and humans. He is not some kind of angel or demigod, but he is a genuine mediator between God and humans because he has his being on both sides. He is the God-Man.

Some Christians prefer to begin their study of Jesus Christ by first of all viewing him as God and then going on also to show that he is human as well. This descending type of Christology takes great care to point out that indeed Jesus Christ possesses the divine prerogative; he indeed is God. Other Christians begin their study with Jesus the man and are particularly anxious to teach that Jesus was really human, like other human beings, except for sin. This ascending type of Christology then proceeds to teach that Jesus is not just human, but he is also God as well. These two points of view emphasize that both natures of Jesus Christ are complete and come together in a single person. The divinity of Jesus Christ without his humanity is only part of the picture, just as to view Jesus only from the point of view of his humanity is to have an incomplete picture of him and not as the New Testament and the major

Christian creeds attempt to portray him.

Some Christians have come to believe in the kenotic theory[6] of "self-emptying" concerning Jesus Christ. This theory is based upon a reading of St. Paul's Letter to the Philippians. It hypothesizes that the Son of God laid aside his divine attributes of omnipotence, omniscience, omnipresence, and so on and took on all the limitations of human existence. He literally emptied himself of his divinity when he assumed his humanity and did not reassume his divinity until the time of his resurrection from the dead, after his death on earth. The kenotic theory has especially gained ground among those Christians who espouse an ascending type of Christology. The major good effect it has upon the doing of Christology is that it helps see Jesus more easily as an authentic human being.

B. Jesus the Man

1. *The Historical Jesus.* There were two basic views of Jesus by his contemporaries. Some saw him only as a Jewish man of his time who was a revolutionary within established Judaism. Others with Christian faith, however, viewed him as the God-Man, as was just pointed out. The latter group saw God revealing himself in Jesus Christ.[7] Nevertheless, it is rather universally recognized that the simple historical facts about Jesus cannot be isolated today because the gospels of the New Testament are practically the only sources of information about Jesus that exist. And they are gospels, faith proclamations about Jesus, written by and for Christian believers. Therefore, they are indeed biased in their view of Jesus, since they are religious books based upon religious faith and not intended as objective, critical biographies or histories.

Whereas it is true that there are no pagan references to Jesus during the first century, there are three brief mentions of Jesus shortly thereafter among three Roman writers. They tell us, however, very little beyond the fact that Jesus lived and had a following of people even after he died. These Roman historians were Pliny, Tacitus, and Suetonius.[8] Their works are known to us today, but are not very helpful for giving much information about Jesus, even though they date from the second century.

The early Jewish sources of evidence about Jesus include the Jewish historian, Flavius Josephus, and the Talmud. Josephus limited himself to a couple of general remarks about Jesus in his *Jewish Antiquities,*[9] indicating that even after his crucifixion Jesus' disciples continued to follow his teachings. The Jewish Talmud comprises tradition dating from the first century and speaks rather disparagingly about Jesus as a false teacher who was executed. No biography of Jesus is found among the Roman or the Jewish sources.

Other Christian sources about Jesus, besides the canonical books of the New Testament, include the apocryphal New Testament writings such as the gospels of Peter, Thomas, and Philip.[10] These writings are obviously fictitious, seeking to satisfy pious curiosity and serving to entertain. These false writings are valueless for authenticating the life of Jesus in spite of the fact that since the discovery of the Nag Hammadi library in 1947 the *Gospel of Thomas* has taken on a certain importance in some circles.[11] There is also very little other information about the historical Jesus found in the New Testament. Therefore, the canonical gospels of the New Testament are practically the only sources about the historical Jesus, and it must be remembered that they are faith proclamations written many years after Jesus actually lived on this earth. The other writings of the New Testament are equally biased.

This problem of the historical Jesus was especially studied in the nineteenth century by Christians beginning with David Friedrich Strauss' controversial work in 1835 titled *Das Leben Jesu.*[12] Strauss was a professor at the University of Tübingen in Germany and he attempted to point out that a critical life of Jesus does not exist outside of the gospels in the New Testament. These gospels were not meant to be either biographies or histories of Jesus. They are proclamations of "the good news of salvation." They contain the glad tidings of what Christians believe God has done for them through Jesus Christ. In more contemporary times, biblical theologians such as Albert Schweitzer[13] and Rudolf Bultmann[14] have attempted to further this train of thought about Jesus and the gospels. Furthermore, it is maintained that the gospels themselves did not come into existence until at least some thirty years or so after the death of Jesus.[15] The message of Jesus was remembered and passed along orally in the primitive Christian community until it was finally written down by the evangelists, each of whom had his own reasons for writing.

There is no question among Christians or non-Christians about the historicity of Jesus. He is universally accepted as an historical figure. If not, Christian beliefs and teachings would make no sense at all. The real question is whether these beliefs and teachings can be taken seriously and can help people give purpose to their lives. In attempting to come to grips with these beliefs and teachings, the canonical, authoritative writings of the New Testament, especially the gospels, become normative while making interpretations. Interpretations there are indeed, since within the United States alone, there are nearly two-hundred different Christian denominations, [16] each maintaining its own understanding of the Bible.

2. *The Life of Christ presented in the New Testament.* In all four gospels, those according to Matthew, Mark, Luke, and John, Jesus is understood as the Messiah or Christ, the promised one. These gospels do help to reconstruct a life of Jesus and it is this writer's intention to isolate some of the major episodes from that life.

a. *The Nativity.* Jesus was born somewhere between 6 and 4 B.C., at least before the death of Herod the Great in 4 B.C. Whereas it may seem Jesus Christ absurd to state that Jesus was born in the era before Christ, the monk in the Middle Ages who first determined our present calendar dating events from the birth of Jesus made a miscalculation. His calendar was about 4-6 years off, and it remains so until today. While examining the synoptic gospel accounts of the birth of Jesus, it is immediately noticed that Mark's account of the gospel has nothing to say on the subject. Because Mark's Gospel is viewed by many to be the oldest of the gospels as we now have them, some biblical scholars have concluded that the stories surrounding the birth of Jesus are probably legendary. However, both Matthew[17] and Luke[18] do have detailed narratives of the birth.

Both the account of the birth of Jesus found in Matthew's and Luke's statements of the Gospel of Jesus Christ teach that Jesus was born of a virgin named Mary. The Gospels of Mark and John and the writings of Paul in the New Testament make no mention of the virgin birth. Some Christians, therefore, do not believe in the virgin birth of Jesus Christ. They claim that there are many myths of virgin births found in pagan and non-Christian religions and that such an idea encourages Christians to think of Jesus Christ as a kind of demigod, like Achilles or Hercules. Further, the opponents of belief in the virgin birth claim that such a teaching takes away from the true humanity of Jesus. If he was truly human,. he must be thought of as having a fully normal human conception.[19]

Those Christians who accept the belief in the virgin birth of Jesus counter these arguments by asserting that it is not a question of biology here. It is a question of theology and the doctrine of the virgin birth of Jesus is meant to point to his origin in God by God's initiative and not by a male's procreative efforts.[20] Both Matthew and Luke make specific reference to the action of the Holy Spirit with regard to the virgin birth. But this action of the Spirit does call for the free response of a woman,

Mary, who gave it with the words: "Let it be done to me according to your word" (Lk. 1:38). For many Christians, the place and function of Mary are extensions of Christological doctrine and are generally called Mariology, especially by Roman Catholic, Eastern Orthodox, and Anglican Christians.

Therefore, with reference to the birth of Jesus as it is depicted in Matthew and Luke, he was born of a virgin in the city of Bethlehem during the reign of Herod the Great who died in 4 B.C.[21] He was born a Jew in rather humble surroundings in Palestine and his birth was accompanied by unusual visitors, including shepherds from the region and also Wise Men from the East. According to Matthew's account, his birth caused Herod to slaughter the male children in and around Bethlehem who were two years old or under because Herod was afraid that his rule would be challenged by this child who was described as "the king of the Jews."[22] To elude Herod's massacre, the holy family, Jesus, Mary and Joseph, her husband, escaped to Egypt until the death of Herod.[23] They then returned to Nazareth, Jesus' boyhood home.

b. *The Baptism of Jesus.* The fact that Jesus was baptized cannot really be doubted by Christians because it would have been embarrassing for his disciples to admit that Jesus was baptized.[24] After all, he was the sinless man who was also God. The story of Jesus' baptism would not have been told unless, in fact, it had happened and indeed was well known among his disciples. Very little in general is known of Jesus' youth. The only glimpse of it occurs when he is twelve years old and is depicted studying the Jewish Law in the Temple at Jerusalem. He perhaps was being admitted to the state of "Son of the Law" *(Ben Torah)* and from then on regarded as an adult religious Jew.[25]

The question that Christians have had to wrestle with throughout the ages is the problem of deciding why Jesus was baptized. Certainly sinless Jesus who was God's own son did not need to be baptized by his cousin, John the Baptist, in the Jordan River. John the Baptist is considered by many Christians to be the immediate forerunner of Jesus and the last of the biblical prophets. Christian writers have suggested many different reasons for the baptism of Jesus. 1) He was baptized to signify that this was the moment of his acceptance of his role and mission as the Messiah, the Christ. 2) He was baptized in order to more closely identify himself with his sinful and repentant people. 3) He was baptized to signify his anointing as king of the new kingdom. 4) He was baptized as an example for others to follow in turning away from their sins. 5) He was baptized to identify himself and his teachings with the ministry already begun by

John. Whatever the reason(s) might have been, Christians refer to the baptism of Jesus as the beginning of his public life, distinguishing approximately the first thirty years of his private life on earth from the rest of his life, which generally is thought to have lasted about three years. Certainly Jesus' divine character is attested to at the time of his baptism according to the words that are heard and the sign perceived: "And when he came up out of the water, immediately he saw the heavens opened and the Spirit descending upon him like a dove; and a voice came from heaven, 'Thou art my beloved Son; with thee I am well pleased'" (Mk. 1:10-11).

c. *The Temptations of Jesus.* After his baptism, Jesus spent a total of forty days in the wilderness preparing for his public life of preaching and teaching the people. At that time Jesus was tempted by Satan.[26] Satan or the Devil are names in traditional Christian belief for the power of evil in the world. Some Christians believe in a personal Satan and employ certain rituals known as exorcism designed to eradicate Satan's power. Other Christians view Satan not in a personal sense, but only as referring to a spiritual, mysterious, and evil power outside of human beings.[27] The idea of a personal Satan generally discerns the Devil or Satan[28] as a fallen angel who rebelled against God and led a revolt in heaven until the Devil and his followers were cast out of heaven. The Devil's followers then are generally referred to as demons. In the New Testament, the Devil is spoken of in a personal sense as he tempts Jesus three times.

The first temptation, turning stones into bread, Jesus overcame by asserting that there is much more to human existence than the material side. By indicating that he is not a materialistic Messiah, he quoted from the Old Testament Book of Deuteronomy[29] that: "Man shall not live by bread alone, but by every word that proceeds from the mouth of God" (Mt. 4:4).

The second temptation, leaping off the top of the Temple in Jerusalem, was the temptation to use his power to perform a miracle for his own gain and thereby impress the crowds. In overcoming this temptation, Jesus rejected all types of magic and hocus pocus with regard to the Christian faith implying that what is important is faith in God. He thus refused to be a supernatural magician, so to speak.

The third temptation, using sinful means to gain the kingdoms of the world, was the temptation to worship creation, Satan, over and above the creator. Jesus forcefully also rejected this temptation with the words: "Begone, Satan! for it is written, 'You shall worship the Lord your God and him only shall you serve'" (Mt. 4:10), again quoting from the Book of Deuteronomy.[30] Resisting and rejecting all of these temptations from the devil at the beginning of his public life, Jesus emerges victorious and shows forth his single mindedness and sinlessness. Moreover, as God, sin would be incompatible for him. But he was truly human as well.

d. *The Miracles of Jesus.* As Jesus went about preaching the gospel, he confirmed his teachings in that regard by performing miracles. In the New Testament, these miracles are described as signs, wonders, mighty works and powerful deeds.[31] They show forth the power of God through the works of Jesus. Customarily, a miracle is thought of as God intervening in the natural world in such a way that the end result appears to be contrary to or outside of the known laws of nature. However, many contemporary Christians think that miracles are not at all contrary to nature, but only contrary to what humans know about nature at any given time. Whereas some Christians accept the miracles attributed to Jesus in the gospels literally, others question their authenticity and claim that the miracle stories in the New Testament are merely a more primitive way of expressing Christian beliefs about Jesus. Moreover, some Christians insist that Jesus could not have performed miracles because miracles are scientifically impossible.[32] Yet there is no doubt that the gospels attribute to Jesus the power to do supernatural things. He is described as turning water into wine, healing the sick, casting out demons, calming a storm, bringing people back to life who had died, and so on. Whether he actually did these things is, however, much debated in the Christian community. The major question in this discussion is not whether one believes Jesus performed miracles or not, but whether one believes this man was the Son of God and the Messiah or Christ.[33]

Of all the miracles attributed to Jesus, his healing miracles are the more numerous. There are only three instances recorded in the gospels of Jesus raising the dead to life and about five nature miracles, such as the calming of a storm, and so on. In all of these healing miracles, faith is of the utmost importance. Jesus at all times attempts to keep his miracles in perspective, seeing them not as proofs for his divinity, but rather as signs of God's presence and power in the world, especially for those who believe in him. Nowhere did he teach that people are saved through miracles. As a matter of fact, Jesus is quoted as saying through Abraham: "If they do not hear Moses and the prophets, neither will they be convinced if someone should rise from the dead" (Lk. 16:31). It would seem, therefore, that faith precedes miracles and Jesus did not hope to attract disciples to himself by merely performing miracles. Yet these same miracles also serve to teach that the promised messianic age has indeed arrived.

e. *Jesus as Teacher/Rabbi.* According to the Gospel of Mark: "After John was arrested, Jesus came into Galilee, preaching the gospel of God, and saying, 'The time is fulfilled, and the kingdom of God is at hand; repent and believe in the gospel'" (Mk. 1:14-15). Jesus traveled especially through the region of Galilee proclaiming the good news of salvation and he taught not only directly but also by his example. One of the more common means that Jesus used to teach his followers or disciples[34] was by means of parables. These parables were stories employed by Jesus to illustrate the truths that he intended to teach. He taught as one who possessed teaching authority, and crowds of people flocked to listen to him.[35] He especially taught about the kingdom of God and said that it was at hand.[36] He compared God's kingdom to a grain of mustard seed, which although very small when it is first sown in the earth, subsequently grows into a large shrub or tree.[37] He also used the image of leaven mixed with flour or meal to teach the future growth of the Kingdom of God.[38]

The kingdom that Jesus proclaimed was different from the kingdom foretold by the prophets of the Old Testament and the Jewish interpretation of the prophets. The Old Testament had predicted a materialistic kingdom that would bring about the national vindication of Israel as a nation through the instrumentality of an "anointed one" or Messiah of God.[39] Jesus made it clear to his followers that the Kingdom of God is a spiritual one. Especially is this seen in the words of Jesus when he was asked by the Roman governor, Pontius Pilate, if he were the king of the Jews and Jesus replied: "My kingship is not of this world; if my kingship were of this world, my servants would fight, that I might not be handed over to the Jews; but my kingship is not from the world" (Jn. 18:36). However, even his own disciples did not understand him on this score because after his resurrection from the dead they asked him if he was now going to restore the kingdom of Israel. Jesus replied: "It is not for you to know times or seasons which the Father has fixed by his own authority. But you shall receive power when the Holy Spirit has come upon you; and you shall be my witnesses in Jerusalem and in all Judea and Samaria and to the end of the earth" (Acts 1:7-8).

While denying the materialistic and nationalistic aspects of the Kingdom of God, Jesus did emphasize the religious aspects of God's rule. He taught that God should indeed rule over people's minds and hearts and that human beings should acknowledge this rule. In this context, Jesus spoke of a person's need to be accepted and forgiven by God for his/her sins, and also what should then characterize this God-given life that the person possesses. Jesus' famous Sermon on the Mount[40] perhaps best characterizes how people are to live in this loving relationship with God and with one another. The question about various Christian views concerning the presence of the Kingdom of God will be studied in a future chapter dealing with the church, the kingdom, and eschatology, the study of the last or end times.

f. *Jesus as the Center of Controversy among the Jews.* Because Jesus taught on his own authority[41] and also because of his great popularity,[42] certain factions within established Judaism saw him as a threat to orthodoxy. At the time of Jesus, Judaism was divided into several major sects or political parties. Although Palestine was under the control of the Romans, the Jews themselves were divided with regard to their attitude toward Roman rule and their Jewish religious beliefs. The major Jewish sects and political groups during the Roman period of Jewish history included those called the Sadducees, the Pharisees, the Essenes, and the Zealots.[43] The Sadducees comprised the landed aristocracy and the priesthood. They were the party of the temple, the priesthood and the court. They were both religiously and politically conservative and counseled cooperation with Rome. They accepted only the written word of the Mosaic Law (*Torah/Pentateuch*) and opposed all new interpretations of it. They were possibly named after Zadok, the high priest at the time of King Solomon, and occupied the majority membership on the Sanhedrin, the chief judicial council or supreme court of the Jews, at the time of Jesus. They did not believe in the resurrection of the dead nor the existence of angels. They embraced the traditional Jewish idea of Sheol for those who had died. Sheol was the gloomy and shadowy underworld for departed spirits.

The Pharisees were the religious liberals who sought to interpret the Law in the light of the times. Their name came from the Hebrew word *parush* meaning "separated" or "separatist." They were apparently successors of the *Hasidim* (pious Jews) who joined with the Maccabees in their religious revolt against the Seleucid Syrians in the second century B.C. The Pharisees comprised the party of the Bible (TaNaK)[44] and the synagogue. They accepted such beliefs as the resurrection of the dead, the existence of angels and the immortality of the soul. The conflict between the Pharisees and the Sadducees is readily apparent in the New Testament.[45]

The Essenes were monastic-type Jews who had dropped out of the mainstream of Jewish society and lived in communes waiting and preparing themselves for what they believed would be the imminent coming of the Messiah. They mainly believed that the rest of Jewish society was corrupt and that is why they became dropouts from that society. They engaged in ascetical practices one of which consisted of frequent ritual washing of themselves signifying their attempt to prepare themselves interiorly for the reception of the Messiah. Many also engaged in following the discipline of celibacy in their lives as well.

A fourth group of Jews were those called the Zealots. They essentially were a largely unorganized group of Jewish patriots who in no way were going to accept and attempt to live under foreign domination and control of their country. They were from the party of the Pharisees but broke away because they found them too pacifistic in their dealings with the Romans. Some hold that the Zealot party was formed at the time of the revolt of Judas of Galilee against the enrollment and taxation of citizens under Quirinius, the Roman governor of Syria in the first century A.D. The Jewish historian, Flavius Josephus, referred to them as comprising "the fourth philosophy," meaning the fourth major group in Judaism distinct from the Sadducees, Pharisees and Essenes. The members of this group were probably very instrumental in inciting the Jews in the "Great Rebellion" against Rome between 66-73 A.D. After the Romans destroyed the city of Jerusalem while putting down this Jewish rebellion, the Zealots were able to hold out against the Romans for three more years at a fortress called Masada where they chose to commit mass suicide in 73 A.D. rather than capitulate to the Romans.

Of all of these groups, it seems that the major enemies of Jesus came from the Pharisees whom Jesus especially condemned for their hypocrisy and insincerity. Because of their intense interest in the very letter of the law,[46] they had by and large fallen into an empty legalism with reference to traditional Jewish belief. In fact, Jesus addressed some of his harshest words against this particular group of Jews:

> Woe to you, scribes and Pharisees, hypocrites! for you are like whitewashed tombs, which outwardly appear beautiful, but within they are full of dead men's bones and all uncleanness. So you also outwardly appear righteous to men, but within you are full of hypocrisy and iniquity. (Mt. 23:27-28)

In recent years, however, many writings have appeared to indicate that there were other sincere Pharisees as well. Nevertheless, we have the word, pharisaical, that has come into the English language meaning phony, insincere, or hypocritical derived from the Pharisees of Jesus' time. Indeed Jesus, in his teachings, does come down very hard upon religious phoniness, insincerity, and hypocrisy.

Because Jesus was acting contrary to the established authoritative interpretations of the Jewish Law, he was condemned by his enemies. These conflicts ranged from Sabbath observance[47] to eating with sinners.[48] In every instance, Jesus gave his own interpretation of the Law and indicated that human need takes precedence over the Law itself. Nonetheless, his enemies were intent upon destroying him. They charged that he was leading the people astray by his teachings and because he was so very popular as a preacher and teacher, he needed to be eliminated.

g. *The Petrine Creed.* As Jesus' ministry progressed, one day as he was walking along with his disciples, he put to them the following question:

> "Who do men say that I am?" And they told him, "John the Baptist; and others say, Elijah; and others one of the prophets." And he asked them, "But who do you say that I am?" Peter answered him, "You are the Christ." (Mk. 8:27-30)

This confession of faith by Peter that Jesus is the Christ or the Messiah has become the cornerstone of the Christian faith. Some Christians refer to Peter's affirmation as the first Christian Creed. This belief that Jesus is the Christ takes up the long Jewish expectation that God will anoint someone to turn things around for the Jews. Especially was Messianism rampant among the Jews during ages of domination and persecution. At the time of Jesus, many individuals were claiming this divine sanction, and history has recorded a whole series of false Messiahs during this pessimistic Roman period.[49]

However, the fact that a disciple of Jesus could actually view him as the Messiah shows that his teachings and example convinced many of his followers. It did not seem to matter that he was different from the expected mold. He was getting through to them and indeed was inaugurating the Messianic age. Centuries later Christians still affirm in their faith commitment that Jesus is the Messiah and, therefore, his teachings take on a preeminence in their lives.

h. *The Transfiguration.* According to Mark's Gospel, about six days after this Petrine confession of faith, Jesus took three of his disciples, Peter, James, and John up a mountain and was transfigured before them.[50] There also appeared Elijah and Moses, and again a voice was heard from a cloud attesting to Jesus' divine sonship. This incident has been explained by some as a post-resurrection experience that his disciples had read back into the story of Jesus' life on earth. Others attempt to describe it in terms of a myth or hallucination.[51] However, the Synoptic Gospels place the account within the life of Jesus as they present it and it appears as a genuine religious experience. The disciples of Jesus receive confirmation, as it were, of their belief that he is the divine Messiah. At his transfiguration, the divinity of Jesus shone forth through his humanity. Furthermore, his continuity with the prophets is indicated insofar as he is identified with Elijah and Moses. The heavenly voice that is heard also testifies to his divinity. He is indeed the God-Man, the foretold and expected Messiah.

i. *The Passion and Death of Jesus.* Having succeeded in their efforts to have Jesus arrested, the leaders of the Jews in Jerusalem convinced the Roman authorities that Jesus was subversive to their rule in Judea and that he had blasphemed by claiming to be the Christ. The punishment for blasphemy, according to Jewish law, was death. Ordinarily, one who was condemned on the charge of blasphemy was stoned to death by the Jews,[52] but because they were under Roman rule, the Jews could not of themselves order the death sentence. The charge of treason was, therefore, added by the Jews when they brought Jesus before the Roman governor, Pontius Pilate. This was based upon Jesus' teachings about the Kingdom and his kingship. Although Pilate was disinclined to condemn Jesus to death, he capitulated to the will of the crowd and ordered that Jesus be put to death by crucifixion.[53]

The sufferings and death of Jesus are truly historical in a very real sense. They comprised a publicly observable event. Jesus was executed at a place called Golgotha, which means the place of the skull, whence we get the English word Calvary from the Latin word for skull, *calvaria*. Jesus was nailed to a cross and died slowly, probably by gradual strangulation, between two thieves who had been condemned to die. Jesus was indeed truly human. He really did die on the cross. Because of the place that Christians believe the cross occupies in their own salvation, the cross has become a major symbol for Christians throughout the years. What Christians believe Jesus accomplished for them by his death on the cross will be the topic for a future chapter concerning reconciliation.

j. *The Resurrection of Jesus.* According to Jewish law, the Sabbath was to begin at sunset, and so the burial of Jesus had to be completed quickly since it was already the middle of the afternoon when he was declared dead.

All four of the gospel accounts agree that a certain Joseph of Arimathea asked Pilate for the dead body of Jesus and buried it in a tomb hewn out of a rock that he had prepared for his own eventual burial. Jesus' body was wrapped in a linen shroud and placed into the donated tomb and a huge boulder was rolled in front of its entrance.[54]

After the Sabbath, on the first day of the week, some of Jesus' disciples came to his tomb to properly anoint his body for burial, as he had been buried with haste the Friday before. These same disciples discovered that the stone had been rolled back and that the tomb was empty. A young man or angel told them that Jesus had risen from the dead. In the words of Mark:

> And he said to them, "Do not be amazed; you seek Jesus of Nazareth, who was crucified. He has risen, he is not here; see the place where they laid him. But go, tell his disciples and Peter that he is going before you to Galilee; there you will see him, as he told you." (Mk. 16:6-7)

Subsequently, Jesus appeared to his disciples many times, and at one time to five hundred of the Christian brethren.[55] Because Christians believe that Jesus rose from the dead on a Sunday, they celebrate Sunday as their Sabbath rather than Saturday, which is the Jewish practice.

The belief in the resurrection of Jesus from the dead is the central doctrine of Christianity. This doctrine symbolizes for Christians that God did accomplish reconciliation for them in Jesus Christ. They basically believe that Jesus has overcome evil for them, and by their union with him, they too can achieve salvation from evil. Their belief in the resurrection has been challenged throughout the years by one or another non-believer, since the resurrection of Jesus was not the publicly observable event that his death was. These objections[56] include: 1)The stolen-body theory which affirms that some of Jesus' disciples stole his body from the tomb. 2) The wrong-tomb idea theorizes that in their haste to care for Jesus' body, the women bypassed Joseph of Arimathea's tomb and stumbled into an empty tomb. 3) The "lettuce theory" claims that a gardener removed the body to keep visitors from trampling his lettuce and other seedlings he had planted around the tomb. 4) The swoon theory is based upon the belief that Jesus did not really die on the cross but simply went into a coma. The coolness of the tomb and the healing qualities of the spices on his body revived him. He removed his burial shroud and appeared to his disciples. But forty days later the infectious wounds got the best of him and he died. 5) The hallucination theory maintains that the women and other disciples of Jesus had hallucinogenic visions of him after his death. Their hallucinations brought about a fever of other visions of Jesus. 6) Finally, the twin-brother theory asserts that a look-alike brother of Jesus assumed the role of Jesus after Jesus' death. Despite all of these and other objections, Christians have persisted in their central belief about Jesus, his resurrection from the dead. In the words of St. Paul, indicating the importance of the resurrection for Christian belief: "...if Christ has not been raised, then our preaching is in vain and your faith is in vain....If Christ has not been raised, your faith is futile and you are still in your sins" (1 Cor. 15:14,17).

The Bible basically speaks of resurrection as an awakening from sleep and the achievement of new life.[57] The concept of resurrection naturally follows from the fact that human beings hope beyond death. No one, it seems, really wants to go out of existence. Being is better than non-being. Yet death cannot be escaped by human beings and so the doctrine of the resurrection offers an answer to this fundamental question of human existence. Christian belief states that it is possible with Jesus to overcome not only evil but death itself and achieve a new life after death. The concept of life after death will be discussed in chapter seven.

The New Testament attempts to teach that Jesus did rise from the dead by pointing out the empty tomb and by enumerating the major appearances of the resurrected Jesus. It is interesting to note that Paul nowhere mentions the empty tomb of Jesus while teaching the resurrection, whereas the gospel accounts do. It seems that the intention of both, however, is to give proof of the resurrection by means of witnesses. Christians generally follow one of four different theories while attempting to make the event of Jesus' resurrection from the dead credible: 1) Some Christians emphasize the empty tomb; 2) others emphasize the appearances of Jesus after his death; 3) still others deny the physical resurrection of Jesus, but claim that his death was efficacious and that the story of the resurrection found in the New Testament means to attest to that belief. They claim too that this bodily resurrection of Jesus is simply a mythological way of asserting his continued presence in the community of believers.[58] However, 4) a very widely held position among Christians combines the first two positions by asserting that Jesus was in fact physically raised from the dead, his body was resurrected, he walked out of the tomb and appeared to his disciples. Because of belief in the resurrection of Jesus, he is a living figure today for Christians. The resurrection of Jesus authenticates his teachings and they have become meaningful for countless numbers of his followers throughout the centuries.

k. *The Ascension of Jesus.* After appearing to and instructing his disciples for some time after his resurrection from the dead, Jesus promised to send them the Holy Spirit to be with them and then he departed from them, ascending into heaven. Many Christians interpret the event of his ascension described in the New Testament[59] as purely a myth reflecting an ancient cosmology based upon a triple-decker view of the universe. Some accept it literally as it is described. But all see in this Christian symbol the triumphant savior who has become the exalted Lord of all. By the same token, Christians look for his return in the future and this remains the primary object of the Christian's hope, even in contemporary times.

This attempt to reconstruct the life of Jesus based upon the New Testament writings included some of the major beliefs of Christians. It is well nigh impossible to separate the beliefs about Jesus from his life itself, as it is presented in that book of Christian faith, the Bible. To believe that the Bible is the Word of God, as Christians do, is also to believe that what is described there has religious meaning. However, the scope of that religious interpretation of the Bible is wide and consequently there are many different varieties of Christian belief. This chapter has endeavored to bring the major positions together.

Notes - Chapter 2

1.Cf. Philip Schaff, *History of the Christian Church*, III (NY: Charles Scribner's Sons, 1910), 618-663.

2.Cf. *ibid.*, 714-733.

3.Cf. *ibid.*, 762-783.

4.Leith, *op. cit.*, 35-36.

5.Cf. also Heb. 1:3; 2:17-18.

6.Cf. Van A. Harvey, *A Handbook of Theological Terms* (NY: Macmillan, 1968), 138.

7.Cf. 2 Cor. 5:18-19.

8.Cf. Daniel J. Theron, *Evidence of Tradition* (London: Bowes and Bowes Ltd., 1957), 11-17; James Peter, *Finding the Historical Jesus* (NY: Harper and Row, 1965), 26-27; and Howard C. Kee, *Jesus in History* (NY: Harcourt, Brace, Jovanovich, Inc., 1977), 45-48.

9.Cf. Theron, *op. cit.*, 5-7; Peter, *op. cit.*, 26; and Kee, *op. cit.*, 42-45.

10.Cf. Edgar Hennecke, *New Testament Apocrypha*, edited by Wilhelm Schneemelcher (Philadelphia: The Westminster Press, 1963).

11.Cf. Elaine Pagels, *The Gnostic Gospels* (NY: Random House, 1979) and Robert W. Funk, Roy W. Hoover, and the Jesus Seminar, *The Five Gospels: The Search for the Authentic Words of Jesus* (NY: Macmillan, 1993). For a critique of these works, cf. Luke Timothy Johnson, *The Real Jesus: The Misguided Quest for the Historical Jesus and the Truth of the Traditional Gospels* (San Francisco: HarperCollins, 1996), 20-27, 97.

12.Cf. David Friedrich Strauss, *The Life of Jesus Critically Examined*, translated from the 4th German edition by George Eliot and edited by Peter C. Hodgson (Philadelphia: Fortress Press, 1972).

13.Cf. Albert Schweitzer, *The Quest of the Historical Jesus* (NY: Macmillan, 1966).

14.Cf. Rudolf Bultmann and Five Critics, *Kerygma and Myth*, edited by Hans Werner Bartsch (NY: Harper and Row, 1961), 1-44.

15.Cf. M. S. Miller and J. L. Miller (eds.), *Harper's Bible Dictionary* (NY: Harper and Row, 1973), 102.

16.Cf. Kenneth B. Bedell (ed.), *Yearbook of American and Canadian Churches 1995* (Nashville: Abingdon Press, 1995), 265-272.

17.Cf. Mt. 1:18-2:18.

18.Cf. Lk. 2:1-21.

19.Cf. Wolfhart Pannenberg, *Jesus--God and Man* (Philadelphia: Westminister, 1968), 141-150.

20.Cf. Karl Barth, *Dogmatics in Outline* (NY: Harper and Row, 1959), 95-100.

21.For a succinct outline of Herod's life based upon Flavius Josephus' *Jewish Antiquities*, cf. Giuseppe Ricciotti, *The Life of Christ* (Milwaukee: The Bruce Publishing Co., 1947), 10-16.

22.Herod had already put to death many people whom he regarded as threats to his rule including one of his wives and some of his children. Cf. G. Ricciotti, *op. cit.*, 13-14.

23.Cf. Mt. 2:19-23.

24.Cf. Mt. 3:13-17; Mk. 1:9-11; Lk. 3:21-22; and Jn. 1:31-34.

25.Cf. Lk. 2:41-52.

26.Cf. Mt. 3:1-11; Mk. 1:12-13; and Lk. 4:1-13.

27.Cf. V. Harvey, *op. cit.*, 216. Cf. also Elaine Pagels, *The Origin of Satan* (NY: Random House, 1995) where Pagels traces the evolution of Satan from its origins in the Hebrew Bible, where Satan is at first merely obstructive, to the New Testament where Satan becomes the Prince of Darkness, the bitter enemy of God and humans, evil incarnate.

28.Satan is derived from a Hebrew word meaning adversary, whereas devil is derived from a Greek word meaning the accuser or slanderer.

29.Cf. Dt. 8:3.

30.Cf. Dt. 6:13.

31.Cf. C. Milo Connick, *Jesus, the Man, the Mission, and the Message* (Englewood Cliffs, NJ: Prentice Hall, 1974), 265.

32.Cf. *ibid.*, 279-284 for a good discussion of these differences.

33.In the words of the Fourth Gospel: "For God so loved the world that he gave his only Son, that whoever believes in him should not perish but have eternal life" (Jn. 3:16).

34.The word, disciple, is taken from a Latin word meaning "learner."

35.E.g., Jesus' popularity is described as follows: "And great crowds gathered about him, so that he got into a boat and sat there; and the whole crowd stood on the beach" (Mt. 13:2).

36.Cf. Mk. 1:15.

37.Cf. Mt. 13:31-32.

38.Cf. Mt. 13:33-34.

39.Cf. Is. 2:2-3; 11:1-2; 35:1-2; 52:9-10; Jer. 31:12; Zech. 14:3,9; 9:9, etc.

40.Cf. Mt. 5:1-7:29.

41.Cf. Mt. 7:28-29; Mk. 1:22; and Lk. 4:32.

42.Cf. Mt. 13:2; Mk. 4:1; and Lk. 5:1-3; 8:4.

43.Cf. Leo Trepp, *Judaism: Development and Life* (Belmont, CA: Dickenson Publishing Co., Inc., 1966), 19-21.

44.The TaNaK refers to the three major parts of the Hebrew Bible, *Torah* (the Law), *Nev(b)iim* (the Prophets), and *Kethuv(b)im*, (the Writings).

45.Cf. Acts 23:6-8.

46.The Pharisees were referred to as *Kedoshim* (saints) by some of the Jewish people. Cf. Leo Trepp, *A History of the Jewish Experience* (NY: Behrman House, Inc., 1973), 60-61.

47.Cf. Mk. 2:23-28; 3:1-6.

48.Cf. Mk. 2:13-17.

49.Cf. John B. Noss, *Man's Religions*, 4th edition (NY: The Macmillan Co., 1969), 406-407.

50.Cf. Mt. 17:1-8; Mk. 9:2-8; and Lk. 9:28-36.

51.Cf. Connick, *op. cit.*, 196-199.

52.Cf. Lev. 24:14-16.

53.Cf. Mt. 27:24-26.

54.Cf. Mt. 27:57-61; Mk. 15:42-47; Lk. 23:50-56; and Jn. 19:38-42.

55.Cf. 1 Cor. 15:1-11 for a basic enumeration of these appearances.

56.Cf. Paul L. Maier, *First Easter* (NY: Harper and Row, 1973), 105-109.

57.Cf. Is. 26:19; Dan. 12:2; 1 Th. 4:13-14; and 1 Cor. 14:20 for the awakening from sleep concept. Cf. also 1 Cor. 15:35-56 for the concept of new life.

58.Cf. R. Bultmann, *op. cit.*, 38-43.

59.Cf. Acts 1:6-11.

Chapter 3

Jesus and Reconciliation

Soteriology is the term in Christian theology that traditionally has been used to study people's salvation. This doctrine is based upon the belief that human beings are sinners and are in need of being saved by God in order to achieve that purpose for which Christians believe God created them. This doctrine also deals with what Christians believe Jesus, as the Christ, accomplished for people by his life and death on earth. Traditionally too, this has been referred to as the doctrine of the atonement. This chapter will be primarily concerned with explaining these basic Christian concepts, along with their various interpretations within the Christian community.

A. Humans as Sinners

1. *The Old Testament.*[1] Already in the first book of the Bible, the Book of Genesis, a story is told about the first human beings created by God, Adam and Eve.[2] This story is couched in much mythological imagery, but in general seeks to teach that, at the beginning of human history, human beings were in a state of friendship with their creator and God. However, due to their disobedience or sin, they became at odds with God and God punished them for their sin. Following the Old Testament story, God sought to renew this loving relationship with humans by choosing to enter into a special union with them through a chosen nation of people, the Israelites.[3] At the same time, while seeking to renew this original relationship, God revealed himself quite extensively to human beings

through his Chosen People, especially through certain actions inaugurated by him, and also through certain people called prophets.

All the time God was seeking to renew sinful creation's good relationship with himself, he also made known a plan whereby this would be effectively done once and for all through the instrumentality of a Messiah. As we have seen in the previous chapter, this Messiah would be the God-Man himself.

Traditionally, the belief that all people are sinners stems from what has been called the concept of Original Sin.[4] The classical understanding of the concept of Original Sin is based upon a reading of chapter three of the Book of Genesis. It posits that since all human beings are descendant from Adam and Eve, all people except Jesus and, in the case of Roman Catholics, the Virgin Mary too, inherit their sin and its consequences. These consequences consist mainly of the belief that human beings have lost the possibility of fulfilling their purpose in life for which they were created by God. They need to be saved from their fallen, sinful state.

Other Christians in more contemporary times, however, reject the classical notion of Original Sin and claim that the concept itself was first taught by St. Augustine in the fifth century to explain the existence of evil in a world created by a good God.[5] Also, since St. Augustine was arguing against a British monk by the name of Pelagius, who was teaching that people could save themselves by doing good works, he cited especially a passage from the New Testament Letter to the Romans,[6] contending that people are sinners and cannot achieve salvation without God's help or grace.[7] At the time of the Protestant Reformation in the sixteenth century, John Calvin[8] and Martin Luther[9] furthered Augustine's notion of Original Sin. The Roman Catholic Church, at its Council of Trent[10] in the sixteenth century, also reaffirmed Augustine's position and in 1968, Pope Paul VI[11] spoke in favor of the traditional belief as well. More recently in the *Catechism of the Catholic Church* it is affirmed that:

> But we do know by Revelation that Adam had received original holiness and justice not for himself alone, but for all human nature. By yielding to the tempter, Adam and Eve committed a *personal sin*, but this sin affected *the human nature* that they would then transmit *in a fallen state*. It is a sin which will be transmitted by propagation to all mankind, that is, by the transmission of a human nature deprived of original holiness and justice. And that is why original sin is called "sin" only in an analogical sense: it is a sin "contracted" and not "committed" -- a state and not an act.[12]

Those Christians who do reject the traditional notion of Original Sin suggest that Augustine's version of Original Sin makes no sense in contemporary times informed especially by science. For example, studies in evolution seem to suggest polygenism rather than monogenism.[13] When human beings evolved, there was not just one man and one woman, but there were many. The biblical story, therefore, should be considered a myth and not real history. As a myth, the story of Adam and Eve points to the basic truth of evil in the world, but it teaches nothing about the inheritance of sin. Furthermore, those who object to Augustine's view claim that he read the Letter to the Romans erroneously because he used a faulty translation of the text found in the Latin Vulgate of Jerome.[14] Instead of reading "sin came into the world through one man in whom all have sinned," it should have read according to the original Greek "sin came into the world through one man and death through sin, and so death spread to all men because all men sinned." Therefore, while denying the biological transmission theory about sin many other Christians do affirm that human beings are sinners, that what has been traditionally referred to as Original Sin is merely a statement of the human condition or the existence of sin in the world.[15] People have sinned in the past and they continue to sin in the present and, therefore, they are in need of God's help while achieving their goal in life, salvation.

2. *The New Testament.* Whereas the idea of universal sinfulness being taught in the Old Testament is a matter of great debate among Christians, the New Testament is quite explicit about human beings as sinners. One of the clearest affirmations of that belief is found in St. Paul's Letter to the Romans:

> For there is no distinction; since all have sinned and fall short of the glory of God, they are justified by his grace as a gift, through the redemption which is in Christ Jesus, whom God put forward as an expiation by his blood, to be received by faith. (Rom. 3:22-25)

These verses not only teach the universality of sin, but they also point out that a person's sin can be taken away through the merits of the Messiah, Jesus.

Throughout both the New and the Old Testament, sin is viewed in terms of disobedience to God's will. This understanding of sin presumes that God has a plan for each person to follow while living one's own life, and that he has manifested this plan somehow to every person. That which indicates to each person how one should live according to this plan is what is generally referred to as conscience. In this sense then, sin is doing something contrary to what one, in one's own judgment, deems to be right.

The New Testament Letter of James describes it thus: "Whoever knows what is right to do and fails to do it, for him it is sin" (James 4:17). When people sin, they are not fulfilling the purpose for which they were created and by doing so are separating themselves from their Creator. Sin involves a breaking off of a personal relationship with God and leads to non-fulfillment and negation. St. Paul expressed these same results: "For the wages of sin is death, but the free gift of God is eternal life in Christ Jesus our Lord" (Rom. 6:23).

Jesus, of course, knew the sinfulness of human beings and that all people are sinners. For example, he spoke of the "adulterous and sinful generation" (Mt. 12:39) and of the "faithless and perverse generation" (Mt. 17:17). He even asserted that: "No one is good but God alone" (Mk. 10:18). In the prayer that he gave his followers to pray when he was requested to do so, Jesus told them to ask God to forgive them their sins while praying.[16] Both Jesus and John the Baptist continually exhorted their followers to repent of their sins and change their way of living.[17] From all of these and other New Testament references, it can easily be concluded that human beings are indeed sinners and in need of reconciliation with their Creator. Christians believe that this reconciliation can be achieved through appropriating to themselves the merits of the life and death of the Messiah, Jesus. This then leads to the Christian doctrine of the atonement.

B. The Doctrine of the Atonement[18]

1. *Definition.* The term, atonement, refers in general to the reconciliation of two parties. Within the word itself are to be found two words indicating the meaning of atonement. These two words are "at one." The doctrine of the atonement, therefore, deals with the Christian belief about how the sinful or broken relationship between God and human beings was healed through Jesus Christ. Whereas before the time of Jesus, people were in an alienated state with reference to God, after the life and death of Jesus, people are able to restore that original loving relationship that God intended when they were created. Humans can thus be at one again with God and live their lives according to God's original design and purpose. All of this is made possible for them by the Christ, Jesus. St. Paul wrote concerning people's sinfulness and Christ's atoning life and death for them:

For there is no distinction; since all have sinned and fall short of the glory

of God, they are justified by his grace as a gift, through the redemption
which is in Christ Jesus, whom God put forward as an expiation by his
blood, to be received by faith." (Rom. 3:22-25)

This basically means that Jesus made up for people's sins by his life and
death on earth, thereby making it possible for them to be reconciled with
God.

This concept of the atonement or reconciliation has been referred to in
different terminology by Christians.   Some Christians, following
especially the teachings of St. Paul in this regard, refer to this experience
of reconciliation as justification or as the achieving of righteousness. St.
Paul used the concept to signify how God went about bringing people
back into an appropriate relationship with himself.[19] This concept literally
means the forgiveness of the sinner.   At the time of the Protestant
Reformation in the sixteenth century, the Protestant Reformers employed
the term justification in their rebuttals against the Roman Catholic position
regarding salvation.[20] Other synonymous terms are regeneration, or being
born again, based upon New Testament language. Jesus is quoted in St.
John's Gospel as saying to Nicodemus that: "Truly, truly, I say to you,
unless one is born anew, he cannot see the kingdom of God" (Jn. 3:3).
These phrases are based upon the Christian belief that just as a person is
born into the physical world, so too must that person be regenerated into
the spiritual world where people are reconciled with God.   Other
Christians refer to the atonement in terms of conversion, indicating a
person's turning away from sin and turning towards God. These Christians
especially like to use the Greek word *metanoia*[21] to express this conversion
because the term indicates both a negative and a positive action of turning
away from sin and a turning toward God. Of course this turnabout is made
possible for human beings by Jesus Christ.   Other terms that are used
include the achieving of salvation, implying that a person has been saved
from sin by God, and redemption, teaching that a person has literally been
bought back from a sinful state through the merits of Jesus Christ. This
means that Jesus' life and death were sufficient to satisfy for all people's
sins. Jesus the Redeemer has brought about the reconciliation of human
beings with God and has made atonement for their sins.

Therefore, this Christian belief in the atonement of Jesus Christ teaches
that, by themselves, humans could not achieve reconciliation with God.
God took the initiative in this respect and made it possible for them to be
reconciled with himself. This was a pure gift or grace on God's part and
not in the least merited by any human person. Again, St. John's Gospel

draws this belief together in a sentence: "For God so loved the world that he gave his only Son, that whoever believes in him should not perish but have eternal life" (Jn. 3:16). What God has done for human beings through Jesus Christ is usually referred to as the objective atonement. Each person's positive acceptance of this through faith is called the subjective atonement.[22] However, not all Christians are in agreement as to what should constitute this acceptance.

2. *Four major theories of the atonement.* Whereas the Christian doctrine of the atonement answers the question why the Son of God became man, suffered, and died, not all Christians are in accord about how it is that Jesus Christ reconciles people with God. There have been various theories in Christian history which have attempted to come to grips with and answer this question.

a. *The Juridical or Legal Theory.*[23] This theory, based upon legal imagery, suggests that God originally created human beings good, but they sinned. These sins constituted an infinite offense because God himself is infinite. Finite humans could not make up for it themselves and God, being a just God, could not simply forgive and forget. He had to punish people for their sins. Therefore, a savior was needed to intercede for sinners, one who could vicariously make up for their sins. This savior, however, must be the equal of God himself in order to remedy this infinite offense. On the other hand, since human beings were responsible for their fallen state, they must in some way pay the debt due to it. Hence, the savior must not only be equal to God, but similar to humans as well. Jesus Christ, who is true God and true man, bore the penalty of sin on behalf of sinners. By his life and death on earth he satisfied the justice of God and made it possible for God to forgive sinners freely. The merit of his sinless life and death on the cross, even though he was innocent of any capital offense, paid the necessary compensation or satisfaction for people's sins. This theory is based upon the notion of vicarious suffering and is referred to as an objective theory since the atonement happens outside of human beings and independent of their acceptance of it or not.

b. *The Sacrificial Theory.*[24] This theory is largely based upon the Old Testament notion of sacrifice and the New Testament Letter to the Hebrews. In Old Testament times an unblemished animal was offered to God in death to satisfy for people's sins. However, this theory states that the sacrifices of the Old Law were imperfect. The lives of the victims that were sacrificed were unstained by sin only because as dumb animals they were innocent. A sinless human was, therefore, needed to appease God's anger. Also the animal victims were sacrificed against their will. In the necessary sacrifice the victim needs to be free from sin and must freely consent to the oblation. In other words, the perfect sacrifice must find the priest and the victim to be the same person. Jesus Christ had all of these qualifications.[25] Therefore, the sacrificial theory is also an objective, vicarious type of theory of the atonement. Jesus, by his life of perfect human obedience and self-surrender, offered to God, through death, the perfect sacrifice, achieving universal expiation for people's sins.

c. *The Subjective, Moral, Humanistic, or Exemplar Theory*.[26] Especially since the nineteenth century and the theology of Schleiermacher,[27] Ritschl,[28] and Rashdall,[29] has this theory of the atonement been popular among more liberal minded Christians. This theory suggests that Jesus was a perfect man and gave to human beings an example to follow. His human life revealed to people God's great love for them in a way which has made them repent of their sins. The effect of the atonement and the change brought about by it become efficacious when a person contemplates God's great love for that person and is stirred thereby to repentance. This theory is based upon a subjective appropriation of God's love understood in terms of Jesus Christ's life and death. This love becomes apparent from reflection upon Jesus' words: "Greater love has no man than this, that a man lay down his life for his friends" (Jn. 15:13). This subjective theory suggests that Jesus is only an example and nothing more. His life and death merely symbolize God's love and are not efficacious acts in themselves, as was suggested by the other two theories. It is up to humans themselves to achieve reconciliation, having been moved by the example of Jesus' life.

d. *The Classical, Dramatic, or Victory Theory*.[30] This theory envisions the atonement in terms of a great battle. Advocates of this theory claim that it is especially taught in the Letters of St. Paul in the New Testament.[31] The early Church Father, Irenaeus, furthered this notion as did Martin Luther in the sixteenth century.[32] There is a large scale war in the universe between God and the forces of evil. Human beings have fallen into the grip of these evil forces by misusing the freedom given to them by God. Jesus the Savior comes into this situation and does battle against these evil powers in order to show God's love for people and to liberate them from the Devil's clutches. With the cross of Jesus comes the overwhelming victory over Satan. The Resurrection of Jesus is the teaching that Satan, in fact, has been decisively defeated and Jesus is the victor. He has brought about human beings' deliverance and has given new life to them, having delivered them from the kingdom of darkness and broken the power of Satan over people. This theory too is an objective theory and utilizes the concept of vicarious atonement, Jesus acting in place of and for human beings.

These four theories of the atonement all attempt to grapple with the question of just what Jesus did for the human race. All of them indicate that although the atonement was a once-and-for-all event, it is presented anew in each age and continues in the community of faith, bringing people and God together. The atonement becomes relevant to people in each age insofar as they accept what Jesus Christ has done for them. This is a matter of faith and commitment to the Christian way of life. Most Christians recognize that the work of reconciliation applies to and is available to all people. To accept it is a matter of Christian conversion.

C. Sanctification

Whereas the Christian doctrine of justification deals with a person's acceptance by God into a loving relationship, even though that person is a sinner, the doctrine of sanctification deals with the positive growth of that good and loving relationship. As a matter of fact, the concepts of justification and sanctification are inseparable. Justification, in effect, is that which God does for people; sanctification involves that which God does in people after justification has occurred. Both justification and sanctification demand a person's free response and commitment. God does not act against any person's free will in that regard.[33]

1. *Definition.* The English word, sanctification, is taken from the Latin word, *sanctus,* which means holy. Traditionally, the word has been used to describe the new status or supernatural life that a person receives from God after having been justified. This helps that person achieve the supernatural end of human life which is sanctity. Some Christians refer to this phenomenon as the life of grace, others as achieving righteousness or new life. Still others describe this phenomenon in terms of "being saved." All Christians indicate, however, that the impetus for living this "new life" continually comes to the justified person through the action of the Holy Spirit. All are called to perfection or sanctity and this doctrine of sanctification deals specifically with how a person is able to achieve this goal.

2. *Christian Perfection.* In the context of his Sermon on the Mount, Jesus enjoined his followers with these words: "You, therefore, must be perfect, as your heavenly Father is perfect" (Mt. 5:48). Since that time, Christians have mulled over and argued about the meaning of these words. Some have claimed that Jesus was only referring to the future life after the

grave by using these words. Others have insisted that Jesus was teaching in terms of Christian obligation and possibility for this life. Still others have believed that perfection consists of living a life of perfect love which is not possible in this life except for the saints. Perhaps the more commonly accepted interpretation of these words of Jesus has been that Jesus has taught the ideal to his followers that God alone is perfect, as he indicated elsewhere.[34] Nevertheless, the Christian is always to strive for this perfection and yet still remains a sinner. The goal then is rather elusive but at the same time it inspires people to cooperate with the action of the Holy Spirit in their lives while seeking their supernatural goal. Even though a person has received justification from God, that person still remains a sinner capable of sinning.

Throughout its history, Christianity has witnessed the rise of many different schools of spirituality.[35] These different points of view all have the purpose of attempting to teach the Christian various ways to strive for perfection. They have included both the Christian's individual relationship with God, as well as the relationship with God through the Christian community. They involve the practice of Christian asceticism which includes spiritual discipline and practices to help people keep the proper Christian perspective in their lives.[36] Some have emphasized the practice of poverty; others have stressed the practice of self-denial; others have taught evangelistic practices; still others have emphasized the practical side of Christian love; some too have counseled celibacy; some also have sought union with God through prayerful meditation and contemplation; still others have sought to get closer to Jesus by seeking to identify intimately with the Virgin, Mary, his mother; some Christians have sought to lose themselves in the Lord by frequent and eloquent practices of ritual and worship; others have sought to get closer to the Lord, Jesus, especially by making pilgrimages to the hallowed Christian shrines; many Christians seek to become more perfect through their work in the secular world, attempting to make Christian principles live in the world at large; still other Christians practice Christian spirituality by particularly trying to develop the special gifts or charisms that they possess from the Holy Spirit. These and other schools of spirituality, including combinations of those listed above, all have the same goal, to achieve Christian perfection. All can point to interpretations of the words and deeds of Jesus found in the New Testament as precedent for their practices.

The classical spiritual disciplines included the practices of obedience, simplicity, humility, frugality, generosity, truthfulness, purity and agapéic love. But whereas, in former times, Christian schools of spirituality tended to emphasize attempts to get out of the world to reach union with God, more contemporary types of spirituality are inclined to look upon the world as the place for genuine human encounter with God. There seems to be a revival of panentheistic thought in Christian circles in modern times whereby Christians are attempting to seek God through his created world, believing that God is in everything.[37] The world was created by God and reconciled to him through Jesus Christ. Therefore, because the world is God's, people encounter and praise God when they praise his world. People serve God when they deal with the things of the world rightly and properly.[38]

This worldly spirituality teaches that obedience to God and his service take many different forms. Among these are such things as reverence and care for the ecological balance in the world; fighting against the demons of hunger, disease, and ignorance; working for the brotherhood and solidarity of all peoples; attempting to overcome prejudice and discrimination; and so on. The true force behind this worldly spirituality is the practice of Christian love. The Christian virtues that Christians believe put them in direct contact with God are the theological virtues of faith, whereby they accept God's gift of salvation; hope, whereby they trust the promises they believe God has made to them; and love, whereby they seek to live their Christian lives in the world, realizing that the law of love summarizes the Christian ethic. In the words of Jesus, replying to the question concerning which is the great commandment in the Law, he said:

> You shall love the Lord your God with all your heart, and with all your soul, and with all your mind. This is the great and first commandment. And a second is like it, You shall love your neighbor as yourself; On these two commandments depend all the law and the prophets. (Mt. 22:37-40)

Many Christians today are inclined to pray to God with their eyes open, rather than withdrawing from the world.[39] They appear to be attempting to penetrate through the world itself to God, realizing especially that: "God is love and he who abides in love abides in God and God in him" (1 Jn. 4:16). The modern martyr and theologian, Dietrich Bonhoeffer, has done much to influence contemporary Christians in this regard. He described Jesus as "the man for others."[40] Many Christians consequently seek in their spiritualities to imitate Jesus by being obedient to God's will and give of themselves to others in love. As Bonhoeffer wrote from his prison cell in Germany:

To be a Christian does not mean to be religious in a particular way, to make something of oneself (a sinner, a penitent, or a saint) on the basis of some method or other, but to be a man -- not a type of man, but the man that Christ creates in us. It is not the religious act that makes the Christian, but participation in the sufferings of God in the secular life.[41]

Perhaps St. Paul best sums up this attitude of many Christians toward Christian perfection in the world today with these words:

If I speak in the tongues of men and of angels, but have not love, I am a noisy gong or a clanging cymbal. And if I have all faith, so as to remove mountains, but have not love, I am nothing. If I give away all I have, and if I deliver my body to be burned, but have not love, I gain nothing. (1 Cor. 13:1-3)

Notes - Chapter 3

1.For a good overview of the biblical notion of sin, cf. Albert Gelin and Albert Deschamps, *Sin in the Bible* (NY:, Desclée, 1964).

2.Cf. Gen. 1-3.

3.This story begins to unfold with God's revelation to Abraham beginning in Gen. 12.

4.Cf. Marc Oraison et al., *Sin* (NY: The Macmillan Co., 1962), especially "The Doctrine of Original Sin" by Gustav Giewerth, pp. 111-177.

5.Cf. Herbert Haag, *Is Original Sin in Scripture?* (NY: Sheed and Ward, 1969), 101-102 and Henri Rondet, *Original Sin: the Patristic and Theological Background* (Staten Island, NY: Alba House, 1972), 109-132.

6.Cf. Rom. 5:12.

7.Cf. Piet Schoonenberg, *Man and Sin: A Theological View* (Notre Dame, IN.: University of Notre Dame Press, 1965), 146-153.

8.Cf. John Calvin, *A Compend of the Institutes of the Christian Religion*, ed. by Hugh T. Kerr (Philadelphia: The Westminster Press, 1964), 41-44.

9.Cf. Martin Luther, "Lectures on Romans," *Luther's Works*, ed. by H.C. Oswald, XXV (St. Louis: Concordia Publishing House, 1972), 296-302.

10.Cf. Leith, "The Council of Trent's Decree Concerning Original Sin," *op. cit.*, 404-407. Cf. also J. A. McHugh and C. J. Callan, eds., *Catechism of the Council of Trent for Parish Priests* (NY: Joseph F. Wagner, Inc., 1954), 541-542 and Ludwig Ott, *Fundamentals of Catholic Dogma* (Cork, Ireland: The Mercier Press, Ltd., 1955), 106-114.

11.Cf. *New York Times*, July 1, 1968, p. 1. This news report called Pope Paul VI's pronouncement a new twentieth century creed that he gave at an open-air Mass in St. Peter's Square on June 30, 1968, marking the fifth anniversary of his coronation as pope, the nineteenth centenary of the martyrdom of Sts. Peter and Paul, and the close of the Roman Catholic Year of Faith. Among other restatements of traditional Roman Catholic beliefs, Pope Paul VI reaffirmed Catholic belief in original sin and the need for baptism even of infants.

12.*Catechism of the Catholic Church* (Liguori, MO: Liguori Publications, 1994), 102, §404.

13.Cf. Richard H. Overman, *Evolution and the Christian Doctrine of Creation* (Philadelphia: The Westminster Press, 1967), 155-162 and Ian G. Barbour, ed., *Science and Religion* (NY: Harper and Row, 1968), 159-257.

14.Cf. Rondet, *op. cit..*, 128-129.

15.Cf. *ibid.*, 244-277; Peter De Rosa, *Christ and Original Sin* (Milwaukee: Bruce Publishing Co., 1967), 121-125 and J. S. Whale, *Christian Doctrine* (NY: Cambridge Press, 1966), 52.

16.Cf. Lk. 11:4. Cf. also *infra* p. 113, n. 54.

17.Cf. Mt. 3:2 and Mk. 1:14-15.

18.For this section, cf. Vincent Taylor, *The Atonement in New Testament Teaching* (London: The Epworth Press, 1963); Gustaf Aulén *Christus Victor* (NY: The Macmillan Co., 1961); and D. M. Baillie, *God Was in Christ* (NY: Chas. Scribner's Sons, 1948).

19.Cf., e.g., Rom. 5:19.

20.Cf. Hans Küng, *Justification: The Doctrine of Karl Barth and a Catholic Reflection* (NY: Thomas Nelson and Sons, 1964) where Küng writes on p. 221 that: "Protestants speak of a declaration of justice and Catholics of a making just. But Protestants speak of a declaring just which includes a making just; and Catholics of a making just which supposes a declaring just. Is it not time to stop arguing about imaginary differences?"

21.Cf. Gelin and Deschamps, *op. cit..*, 99, 132, 137-138. Cf. also Bernard Häring, *The Law of Christ*, I (Westminster, Md.: The Newman Press, 1961), 387-419.

22.Cf. Baillie, *op. cit..*, 197-202.

23.Cf. Aulén, *op. cit..*, 81-95. This theory, because of St. Anselm's influential book, *Cur Deus homo*, is often regarded simply as the Anselmian doctrine or the Latin theory.

24.Cf. *ibid.*, 76-78. Because the sacrificial view is so similar to the juridical or legalistic view of the atonement, some authors do not distinguish between them.

25.Cf. Heb. 4:14-5:7.

26.Cf. Aulén, *op. cit..*, 133-142.

27.Cf. Friedrich Schleiermacher, *The Christian Faith*, II (NY: Harper and Row, 1963).

28.Cf. Albrecht Ritschl, *The Christian Doctrine of Justification and Reconciliation* (Edinburgh: Edmonston and Douglas, 1872).

29.Cf. Hastings Rashdall, *The Idea of the Atonement in Christian Theology* (NY: Macmillan, 1920).

30.Cf. Aulén, *op. cit..*, 98-133.

31.Cf. *ibid.*, 61-80.

32.Cf. *ibid.*, 16-35; 101-122.

33.Exceptions to this general Christian belief are found in theories of predestination.

34.Cf. Mk. 10:18.

35.Cf. Paul Hessert, "Christian Life," *New Directions in Theology Today*, V (Philadelphia: The Westminister Press, 1967), 18-41.

36.Cf. Mt. 19:16-22.

37.Cf. C. Hartshorne and W.L. Reese, eds., *Philosophers Speak of God* (Chicago: University of Chicago Press, 1965), 29-57, 233-364, 499-514. The Jewish philosopher/theologian, Martin Buber, was influential in furthering this type of thought especially in his classic *I and Thou* (NY: Charles Scribner's Sons, 1958).

38.For an example of this kind of Christian belief and thinking, cf. Pierre Teilhard de Chardin, *Hymn of the Universe* (NY: Harper and Row, 1961).

39.Cf. Hans Küng, ed., *Life in the Spirit* (NY: Sheed and Ward, 1968), 77-83. For a good application of this method of prayer cf. Elizabeth A. Dreyer, *Earth Crammed with Heaven: a Spirituality of Everyday Life* (NY: Paulist Press, 1994).

40.Cf. Dietrich Bonhoeffer, *Letters and Papers from Prison* (NY: The Macmillan Co., 1962), 237-240.

41.Dietrich Bonhoeffer, *Letters and Papers from Prison*, revised, enlarged edition (London: SCM Press Ltd., 1971), 361.

Chapter 4

Christian Faith

While examining the question of whether or not God as such exists, there are three fundamental belief positions that can be taken. Each is based upon its own preconceived set of presuppositions. First of all, there is the positive belief in the nonexistence of God, which is called atheism.[1] Atheism is a faith option progressively more common in contemporary times, largely because of the existence of pluralistic forces at large in the world opening up religious, non-religious, and even irreligious alternatives for human beings. Atheism has gained much of its momentum and attracted sincere advocates mainly because it is impossible for contemporary people living in a scientific and technologically oriented world to affirm theism or belief in God in the same way as they affirm empirical reality in the physical world about them.

There is also the belief position which decides to remain neutral about the question of God's existence. Agnosticism[2] involves the absence of any decision, one way or another, on this issue. The agnostic affirms that the existence of God is not impossible, but it is improbable for lack of necessary evidence from the agnostic's point of view. This is much more than mere skepticism, which includes the doubting or questioning of either the theistic or the atheistic positions from within an accepted faith context. The agnostic has made the decision on this issue not to decide it one way or another for lack of sufficient evidence.

It is the third alternative of theism, a positive belief in the Christian God, with which this chapter will be concerned. It will not attempt to "prove" this belief, since that is beyond the scope of this volume. The basic presupposition of Christianity is that God does indeed exist and this theistic belief of Christians distinguishes God from creation, but nevertheless views God as the source and sustainer of creation.[3] In this sense then, the Christian God really exists for the Christian and is not just some sort of delusion or other, invented by human beings. On this issue, however, Christians generally graciously admit that God's existence can neither be proven nor disproved except to someone who shares the same set of theistic presuppositions. These presuppositions are in the realm of faith and are incapable of proof as such. As a matter of fact, if it can be proven, it is no longer in the realm of faith, but a part of demonstrated, rational knowledge.[4]

A. Reason Related to Faith

The relationship between reason, especially in terms of science, and religion has not been at all times harmonious over the past centuries. Beginning in the sixteenth century with Copernicus and followed by Galileo in the seventeenth century, the feud between the two disciplines gained momentum, until the present time where there appears to be more or less a standoff. With Copernicus' rejection of the Ptolemaic view of the universe in his *De Revolutione Orbium Coelestium* of 1543 in favor of the heliocentric view, that the sun and not the earth is the center of the solar system, the scientific revolution had commenced.[5] Since that time people have become increasingly more aware that they are the center of their own planet and they have increasingly sought to dominate it through the advancement of science. Galileo sided with Copernicus in his *Dialogo Dei Due Massimi Sistemi Del Mondo* in 1632. However, in 1616, Copernicus' work was placed on the *Index* of forbidden books by the church in Rome, and Galileo was sentenced to imprisonment in 1633, after his work was handed over to the Inquisition. The prison sentence was never imposed, but Galileo was forced to live under house arrest in Siena, Italy before eventually being allowed to return to his hometown. Both Copernicus' and Galileo's conclusions were judged to be heretical since they did not seem to correlate with the accepted interpretation of the Bible by the official church.[6] Nonetheless, the scientific revolution was under way, and in spite of resistance encountered from segments in the Christian church, it gained momentum throughout the seventeenth and eighteenth centuries, which are often referred to as the period of the Enlightenment or the Age of Reason.

By the nineteenth century, scientific method was being applied to human beings, their history and civilization, their social organization, and so on.[7] The Protestant Reformation in the sixteenth century and the further splintering of the Protestant churches themselves helped to free science in the western world from the clutches of the Christian church, and gradually it emerged as a study distinct from any preconceived religious faith positions. Furthermore, the questioning of science brought about a very substantial challenge to the accepted religious concepts. For example, the publication of Charles Darwin's *The Origin of Species* in 1859 about evolution claimed that human origin was due to natural forces existing in the world. Christian beliefs about creation and the theological "proofs" for God's existence from his design in nature were definitely threatened. Karl Marx (1818-1883) basically viewed religion as having been invented by the upper classes in society as kind of an opiate to help keep the lower classes in subservience.[8] He, along with Emile Durkheim (1858-1917) who claimed God was merely society in disguise,[9] did a whole lot to convince many people that religion is of sociogenic, rather than of transcendental origin, as Christian orthodoxy had taught. Further, the father of psychoanalysis and discoverer of the human unconscious, Sigmund Freud (1856-1939), concluded in his studies that religion is none other than a psychological crutch for people to use to help them through the more threatening aspects of their lives. In fact, Freud defined religion as "the universal obsessional neurosis of humanity."[10] Common to all of these "scientific" theories is the belief that God is the creation of human beings themselves, that God has not existence in and of himself. These conclusions very definitely were contrary to orthodox Christian belief and they were and have been answered in one way or another by Christian believers.

In the nineteenth century there were essentially two major types of reactions to these threats and challenges of science whereby Christians attempted to defend their Christian faith. In general, the reaction of the Roman Catholic Church was its attempt to tighten up the dogmatic formulations of the Roman Catholic Church by clearly restating its understanding of Christian beliefs and listing the errors associated with those beliefs. In fact, in 1864, a *Syllabus of Errors* was published by Pope Pius IX condemning those who had been influenced by false beliefs.[11] The accused were labeled as Modernists and there was the attempt by church authorities to search out and excommunicate those who had been positively persuaded by the erroneous beliefs. During the pontificate of Pope Pius X, a form of the Inquisition was re-instituted with the establishment of a secret society called the *Sodalitium Piani* (the Sodality of Pius).[12] Its purpose was to spy on members of the church for the sake of uncovering Modernist tendencies toward heresy. Especially was the Modernist purge of the Roman Catholic Church aimed at testing the orthodoxy of teachers and those in positions of influence and authority in the Roman Catholic Church.

The Protestant reaction in the nineteenth century in general was different from the Roman Catholic attempt to cope with the challenges brought to bear against traditional religious concepts by some scientific circles. Many Protestant churches attempted to adjust to the changing times and ways of thinking brought about by scientific discoveries.[13] Therefore, traditional Christian views were rethought in light of the findings of science in an attempt to rehabilitate Christian orthodoxy. This compromise process, however, was not without its dangers, especially those of rationalism and sectarianism, which in fact did indeed further split the Protestant churches in both the nineteenth and the twentieth centuries.[14]

The relationship between religion and reason or science in contemporary times has pretty much tempered. Each seems to realize that they have their own sphere of competency to operate within and try not to overstep the boundaries within their own realm of endeavor and expertise. For example, it is generally recognized by thinking and believing people today that presuppositionless thinking is impossible.[15] This is true of the scientist as well as of the theologian. There is at least the possibility then that God does in fact exist and that he is not simply the fabrication of human beings. Furthermore, Christians believe that this God has made himself known to humans. The existence or nonexistence of this transcendental God cannot be proven one way or the other, but the Christian believer realizes that one can give motives for one's own belief. The possibility that God does in fact exist forms the basis of the Christian believer's faith, which is then grounded upon past formulations of that faith in the Christian church, as well as upon attempts to make that faith relevant in the contemporary world.[16] The current Christian apologetic then is one based upon the presupposition of faith in the existence of God who can be known, loved, and served in this world. But it also recognizes that this belief lies in the area of faith which goes beyond reason.

Christian theology, therefore, starts from the premise that there is a God and that he can be known because he has revealed himself to human beings. This belief in the Christian God is then reflected upon in the light of not only the experience of the life of faith in the Christian community, but also with the knowledge of how the Christian community has understood and interpreted this faith in the past. This would include that the theologian is aware of the Christian creeds and also the historical tradition of the Christian community itself. Primary in this regard are the basic writings containing the primordial or basic revelation of God upon which the community was founded. These are found in the Christian sacred writings or scriptures, namely, the Bible. Also of importance is Christian tradition which consists of the written and unwritten records, accounts, and interpretations of revelation passed along throughout the years in the community, but not found explicitly in the Bible. The place of tradition, including the teachings of church councils, creeds, and so on, has been debated among Christian theologians throughout the years with regard to the emphasis that it should have upon the theologian's work. Bringing reason to bear, the Christian theologian draws from these many sources while attempting to make Christian beliefs intelligible to the contemporary world. The word, theology, comes from the Greek words *theos* (deity) and *logos* (discourse). The theologian is one who systematically and rationally attempts to clarify Christian faith, employing the tools, generally of philosophy, for giving structure, method, and expression to the work.

Throughout the Christian centuries, however, theologians have not always held the same views on the place that reason should occupy in the doing of theology. These views have varied from extreme rationalism, which claims that reason alone is the only real test of truth to anti-rationalism, which asserts that reason is totally unable to prove or disprove religious beliefs. As a matter of fact, the anti-rationalist position holds that human reason is so corrupt, perverted, and sinful that it can lead one away from religious truth instead of toward it. More often than not, the majority of Christian theologians take the attitude that reason, the power of comprehending, and faith complement one another. In general, however, Protestant Christians tend to distrust human reason more than Roman Catholic Christians do. They hold that human reason is indeed corrupt and limited, but it can act as an instrument of faith, and can only operate at its maximum efficiency when it is illumined by faith. Therefore, from the Protestant point of view, faith always comes first, but it does seek to be understood by human reason.[17]

The Roman Catholic view of the relationship between faith and reason is more optimistic with regard to human reason. For example, it is a dogma of the Roman Catholic Faith that God can be known with certainty through his works by reason alone.[18] Reason has been given to all people as a natural endowment, and although people are sinners, it is not completely corrupt even though it is often obscured and distorted by error. People still can discover much about God by using their reason and where one's reason leaves off, faith takes over. It seems to this writer that the major difference between the traditional Protestant and Roman Catholic views regarding the relationship between faith and reason is one of point of departure. Both positions see them as complementary, but the Protestant view begins with faith and ends up with reason whereas the Roman Catholic view begins with reason and ends up with faith carrying on to the end.

B. Definition of Christian Faith

The Epistle to the Hebrews contains the only definition of faith found in the New Testament: "Now faith is the assurance of things hoped for, the conviction of things not seen" (Heb. 11:1). This is sometimes referred to as the preacher's definition of faith because of the frequent use it has been put to from the Christian pulpit. This definition regards faith as more than an opinion or attitude, but as a conviction and certitude. The "assurance of things hoped for" deals with the notion of salvation discussed earlier. Whereas all visible things are transitory, a person's faith puts that person in contact with invisible and permanent things in God's everlasting kingdom. Therefore, faith is beyond seeing and reasoning. It lies in the realm of dark and unseen certitude. As St. Paul wrote: "We look not to the things that are seen but to the things that are unseen; for the things that are seen are transient, but the things that are unseen are eternal" (2 Cor. 4: 18). While reprimanding Thomas for his disbelief, the resurrected Jesus asserted: "Blessed are those who have not seen and yet believe" (Jn. 20:29). This conviction of faith is grounded in the person of Jesus Christ. It involves an unshakeable confidence in him, not upon certain intellectual arguments or proofs. The Christian confesses that Jesus is the Messiah, one's Lord and Master, and believes that what Jesus has taught is indeed true and efficacious for salvation . Christians reflect Peter's words: "Lord, to whom shall we go? You have the words of eternal life; and we have believed, and have come to know, that you are the Holy One of God" (Jn. 6:68-69). It is this same conviction that Christians have had throughout the years about Jesus and their relationship with him.

Within the history of Christian thought different aspects of faith have been emphasized from time to time. Traditional Roman Catholic theology sought to define faith in terms of mental assent to certain religious truths. This view of faith sought to explain it as an act of the intellect commanded by a person's will.[19] At the time of the Protestant

Reformation in the sixteenth century, the reformers attacked this intellectualistic model of faith and replaced it with the notion that faith is the basic orientation of the total person in terms of abiding trust or confidence in God.[20] Whereas the one view tended to regard faith cognitively, and as the first step toward salvation, the other view was more voluntaristic, seeing all one's activities as expressions of one's basic orientation to God. The cognitive model of faith requires that the believer go on to develop the other theological virtues of hope and charity as well in order to bring faith to its proper fruition. The voluntaristic model claims that faith alone constitutes the accurate and decisive relationship between humans and God and thus its definition would include the notions of hope and charity as well.

In contemporary times, however, Protestants and Roman Catholics are more in agreement with what constitutes faith from the Christian point of view. They all agree that faith is foremost a gift or grace from God, citing the words of Jesus: "No one can come to me unless the Father who sent me draws him, and I will raise him up at the last day.... Truly, truly, I say to you, he who believes has eternal life" (Jn. 6:44,47). Whether to respond or not to this gift of faith involves the freedom of human beings. No one is forced to believe, only invited by God himself to accept and encounter Jesus as one's personal Lord and Savior. The acceptance of this invitation involves principally three intertwined aspects: trust (*fiducia*), knowledge (*assensus*), and commitment (*confessus*).[21] This means that Christian believers, in spite of all evidence to the contrary, have freely willed to place their abiding trust and confidence in God. This involves living in the knowledge and truth of Jesus Christ. It also requires that believers be publicly responsible for their trust and knowledge of this truth in their daily lives. Therefore, faith is not a mere opinion; it involves a once and for all decision and is in the realm of conviction. In this sense then, a temporary believer is really no believer at all and does not know what genuine faith is. The fact that the contemporary definition of faith includes the notion of commitment shows that faith is not a static but a dynamic reality in the life of the believer. There is always motion implied in faith. For example, the ancient Latin Christian creeds usually began with the words: "*Credo in unum Deum.*" The fact that the preposition "*in*" was used with the accusative rather than the ablative case in the Latin language shows that the early framers of these creeds wished to imply the notion of motion in the act of faith of the believer, when the believer confesses: "I believe in one God."

The certitude that believers have from their Christian faith is not the same type of certitude called metaphysical or absolute certitude as is found, for example, in the empirical sciences. Rather, this certitude is practical or religious insofar as the believer possesses an underlying conviction that life is meaningful and worth living. This basic meaning in life is always there, even though at times certain doubts or questions are present. These doubts or questions serve to help deepen the believer's faith in the process. In this regard, Martin Heidegger, the philosopher, has written that: "A faith that does not perpetually expose itself to the possibility of unfaith is no faith but merely a convenience."[22] Paul Tillich echoes these words by stating that: "Serious doubt is confirmation of faith."[23]

As part of a person's whole being, Christian faith is much like the sentiment of love. As love grows, deepens, and seeks to possess the person who is loved, so too does faith broaden in the life of the believer, seeking to possess the person of Jesus himself by participation in his life. To think of faith not as a possession, but rather as a state of being, gives the believer a certain security for living daily life because that person's uncompromising trust has been placed in God, who is Ultimate Reality itself. There is no fear or worry about God going out of existence because that would be contrary to God's very perfection. The tensions of life remain, but the person with Christian faith meets them in a different way from the unbeliever. In this sense, faith is similar to a new pair of glasses. The believer sees things from a different perspective and meaning.

C. The Conversion Process

The conversion process for those embracing Christianity is generally a long and gradual one. The conversion of the great Apostle to the Gentiles, St. Paul, in the New Testament is regarded as the exception rather than the rule in the conversion process. Perhaps the nineteenth century father of modern existentialism, Søren Kierkegaard, makes as good as any attempt to show how a person searches for meaning in life and undergoes the process of Christian conversion. Kierkegaard in his writings analyzes three different stages of existence, including the aesthetic, ethical, and religious levels for individuals facing the question of the meaning of existence.[24]

According to Kierkegaard, the aesthetic stage is described as that level of existence where a person's chief goals are to escape boredom and to fill one's life with new and interesting experiences. This type of life is characterized by a life of immediacy and pleasure. It does not involve haphazard pleasure seeking, and so does involve some self-control. The aesthete follows a kind of "rotation method"[25] as a plan of action to overcome boredom. Moreover, one must seek in this sphere not to get too tied down, either to people or experiences, and become dependent upon them because this will eventually lead to boredom. Therefore, for the aesthete romance can be wonderful, but marriage would be out of the question because of the limitations it would impose upon one's freedom to seek new and interesting experiences. The immediate moment is much more important than long-range commitments. However, after a time, the aesthetic approach to life itself may become boring because the aesthete becomes weary with himself or herself. The playboy or playgirl view of life does not ultimately satisfy the person who may become sick of himself or herself and find that the aesthetic life is without a center and a meaning that lasts and sustains. This leads to a certain melancholy and despair, as the ambience of this stage of existence goes stale and even sour. There comes the realization that a fundamentally different orientation to one's life is needed to save oneself from ultimate self-destruction. The irony of this situation leads the person into the second stage of existence.

Kierkegaard views the ethical stage of human existence to be superior to the aesthetic. To enter this second stage requires that one come to grips with oneself in a way different from the aesthetic stage. This level concentrates on the resolute commitment that is demanded in order to escape from the dangers of the aesthetic life. This commitment is characterized by a sense of duty in one's life whereby one seeks continually to act in a decisive manner. This means that the person on this level of existing needs to anguish over certain choices that are present. Whereas the aesthete's goal was to escape boredom by engaging in novel and interesting experiences where individual choices are not important, the ethical person views each choice with seriousness and a certain amount of anguish. This second stage of existence is characterized, for example, by the life of the married person who is committed to his or her spouse.[26] Continuity and stability come about in one's life through commitment to another person and to the duties demanded by the marriage contract. Having chosen this commitment and striving to deepen it with one's partner in marriage makes a person's life more meaningful and fulfilling. However, because of the importance that the ethical stage places upon the self-sufficiency of the person to do

his or her duty in life, at the same time, human beings are all too aware
that they do not always do their duty nor strive for the ideal. Life indeed
cannot be taken too seriously from the purely rational point of view.
There are many problems that do not have a rational solution to them.
Since people are aware of, at times, shrinking from their duty in life in
the ethical sphere and leaving undone many things that should be done,
they experience a certain guilt. The experience of this guilt can lead a
person to despair that life has meaning much the same way the boredom
of the aesthete can lead to despair. There is a way out of this morass of
guilt and despair, however, and some people do find the way by going
on to the third and final stage of human existence.

The religious stage of existence is characterized by the leap of faith
whereby one affirms one's allegiance to and dependence upon the
transcendent and personal God. This leap of faith places the unique
individual person alone and as a sinner before God himself, who is
known in Jesus Christ. It is Jesus Christ who has redeemed human
beings from sin and who has made it possible for them to achieve peace,
meaning, and eternal life. The religious person is not moved by the
desire merely for enjoyment and novelty nor by purely rationalistic,
ethical duties. Rather, the religious person finds meaning in living a life
of obedience to God by making the leap of faith. Kierkegaard refers to
the Old Testament figure, Abraham, as an example of living in this
sphere.[27] Abraham was willing to sacrifice his son, Isaac, even though
he was not moved to do so by a desire for enjoyment and novelty nor by
abstract rationalistic concepts of duty. Instead, his response was one of
faith in a personal and transcendent God who may direct persons in ways
contrary to the goals of either the aesthetic or rational levels of existing.
If Abraham had remained on the level of reason, for example, he would
have been incarcerated in the ethical sphere. Instead, he made a leap of
faith beyond reason and operated on the religious level, where alone can
ultimate meaning and purpose to one's life be found. It is by living in
faith that one becomes a truly authentic individual. One is aware of
one's own finitude and yet craves for meaning, fulfillment, and
understanding. All of this is found in having made the leap of faith and
living one's life of loving response to God who is love himself.
Authentic existence, according to Kierkegaard, can only be found on this
religious level of existence.

Following Kierkegaard's outline of the three stages of human existence
sheds some light upon the conversion process in general. Certainly when
people confront the more threatening aspects of their existence readily

apparent in such fundamental limiting experiences of life as guilt, suffering, evil, alienation, the threat of death, and the like, they search for an ultimate meaning to existence itself. When one comes to realize that one cannot escape from asking profound questions with regard to one's existence and cannot overcome the anxiety produced by these questions by oneself, one is ready to accept the gift of faith itself. The acceptance of this gift involves a turning away from previously inadequate solutions and a turning towards the ultimately meaningful solution found in the person of Jesus Christ. By encountering this God-Man in a genuine leap of faith beyond oneself and reason itself, the Christian gains peace of mind and a new understanding and appreciation for all areas of life. At the same time, the believer does not dispense with reason, but strives to strike a balance between faith and reason. Faith is a choice and a decision, not an argument nor a debate. Leaps of faith are made in many areas of life such as marriage, the choosing of a career, education, and so on. In fact, most important decisions in life are made by faith informed by a certain amount of known evidence. But, just as the leap of religious faith goes beyond reason, so too do many major decisions people make while thoughtfully leading their daily lives. The ambiguities of daily living remain, but they are viewed in a different light because of the decision the Christian has made. Life does have meaning; it is not absurd. It does have the goal of salvation; it does not end in despair and meaninglessness. With this perspective, the Christian believer goes about his or her activities in the world and has the assurance of his or her faith, which has been placed in that which the Christian believes is truly Ultimate Reality, the God-Man himself.

D. Religion and Religions

The leap of faith that the Christian has made is toward the religion of Christianity. Religion may be defined as that which binds a person to Ultimate Reality. Of course, there are many different religions adhered to by people throughout the world, one of which is Christianity. The question arises, therefore, how Christianity is related to the other religions of the world. It also brings to mind the question of what is the "true" religion. Traditionally, Christians have regarded their religion as the only true religion. However, among many contemporary Christians there is the belief that there is no one true religion as such. A religion is true for that person who professes it.

There are at least four basic attitudes that a Christian can take with respect to the other religions of the world.[28] First of all, there is the absolutist view which is completely intolerant of all other views of Ultimate Reality. This is the belief that the Christian Faith alone is the true religion and that salvation can only be achieved through explicit faith in Jesus as the Christ. Secondly, there is the relativist view which basically affirms that one religion is as good as another. There is a third position that qualifies the relativist view and affirms that there is but one God who has made himself known to people in a variety of ways, encompassed in the religions of the world. For example, the Buddha, Moses, Mohammed, Lao-tzu, and so on, are all to be understood as prophets of the one God. This view adds the dimension of strict monotheism to the relativist position. A fourth view also qualifies the absolutist position by affirming that Jesus Christ is the only mediator between God and humans. Whatever good is found in the other religions of the world ultimately is grounded in the person of Jesus Christ. Therefore, a person can achieve salvation through Jesus Christ without being explicitly aware of him, only implicitly through the authentic teachings of another religion, whatever they might be. This final view distinguishes between implicit and explicit faith. Each is capable of leading to salvation when sincerely embraced by the religious believer.

Whatever the Christian's view is of his or her relationship to believers found among the other religions of the world, Christianity demands sincerity and good will.[29] Jesus stated that: "I am the way, and the truth, and the life; no one comes to the Father, but by me" (Jn. 14:6). However, Christians differ in their belief with regard to how salvation may be accomplished among sincere people of good will, from more uncompromising absolutist positions to extremely liberal relativist positions. Each of the positions taken presents its own problems, but these are worked out again in the light of the presuppositions adhered to by individual Christian believers. As was pointed out above, many thoughtful people have come to the conclusion that faith in an Ultimate Reality is necessary for a truly meaningful existence. However, from the Christian point of view, not all Christian believers are in agreement upon what constitutes this faith, especially as it is related to other prevalent faiths in the world at large. Perhaps the creative tension among different religious believers is no more acutely felt than among those in the United States of America whose Constitution does not embrace any one religion as such. The fact that this freedom of religion has worked well for the citizens of the United States indicates that perhaps, for the healthier religious outlooks, the guarantee of religious pluralism is essential.

Where the intolerance of other religious viewpoints besides the established state religion has existed in history, all too often the authenticity and credibility of that religion has suffered. Extremism always involves a certain impoverishment because it only allows for one side of any given issue to be expressed. Dialogue and acceptance of the fact that religious faith lies in the area of personal choice and freedom can only serve to enhance one's own position, which also relies upon the good will of others.

Notes - Chapter 4

1.For a good exposition of the different stances taken by atheists, cf. William A. Luijpen and Henry J. Koran, *Religion and Atheism* (Pittsburgh: Duquesne University Press, 1971).

2.For an overview of the agnostic position, cf. Paul Edwards, ed., *Bertrand Russell: Why I am Not a Christian* (NY: Simon and Schuster, 1967).

3.God's action in history as preserver and guide of creation is expressed in the Christian concept of divine providence.

4.The study of the philosophy of religion in general produces the conclusion that arguments for both theism and atheism are inconclusive when put to critical examination.

5.Cf. Alan Richardson, *The Bible in the Age of Science* (London: SCM Press, Ltd., 1964), 9-12.

6.Cf. *ibid.*, 16-18.

7.Cf. *ibid.*, 32.

8.Cf. Karl Marx and Friedrich Engels, *On Religion* (Moscow: The Foreign Languages Publishing House, 1957) reprinted by (NY: Schocken Books, Inc., 1967), 41-42.

9.Cf. Emile Durkheim, *Elementary Forms of Religious Life* (NY: The Macmillan Co., 1963).

10.Cf. Sigmund Freud, *The Future of an Illusion* tr. by W.D. Robson-Scott, rev. ed. by James Strachey, (Garden City, NY: Doubleday and Co., Inc., 1964), 70-71.

11.Cf. B.M.G. Reardon, *Religious Thought in the Nineteenth Century* (Cambridge: At the University Press, 1966), 1-3, 30-31.

12.Cf. Robert Adolfs, *The Church is Different* (NY: Harper and Row, 1966), 27-30.

13.Cf. Reardon, *op. cit.*, 3-29.

14.Cf. Philip Schaff, *The Principle of Protestantism* (Philadelphia: United Church Press, 1964), 129-155.

15.Cf. James Wm. McClendon, Jr. and James M. Smith, *Understanding Religious Convictions* (Notre Dame, Ind.: University of Notre Dame Press, 1975), 85-114.

16.The Christian creeds symbolize the Christian community's understanding of its faith at any one time in its history. It has been said that the better creeds are those which are the more open-ended, leaving room for further future development.

17.Cf. Karl Barth, *Anselm: Fides Quaerens Intellectum* (NY: Meridian Books, 1962).

18.Cf. Ott, *op. cit.*., 13-14 and *Catechism of the Catholic Church, op. cit.*. §36.

19.Cf. Thomas Aquinas, *Summa Theologica*, II (NY: Benziger Brothers, Inc., 1947), 1179-1180.

20.Cf. Theodore G. Tappert, ed., "The Treatise on Good Works, 1520," *Selected Writings of Martin Luther 1517-1520* (Philadelphia: Fortress Press, 1967), 110-112 et passim.

21.Cf. Karl Barth, *Dogmatics in Outline* (NY: Harper and Row, 1959), 15-34.

22.Martin Heidegger, *An Introduction to Metaphysics*, translated by Ralph Manheim (New Haven: Yale University Press, 1959), 7.

23.Paul Tillich, *Dynamics of Faith* (NY: Harper and Row, 1958), 22.

24.These three stages of existence are described in Søren Kierkegaard's works such as *Either/Or*, 2 vols., translated by David F. Swenson, Lillian Marvin Swenson and Walter Lowrie, with revisions by Howard A. Johnson (Garden City, NY: Doubleday and Co., Inc., 1959); *Fear and Trembling* and *The Sickness Unto Death* translated by Walter Lowrie (Garden City, NY: Doubleday and Co., Inc., 1954); *Philosophical Fragments: or A Fragment of Philosophy* translated by David F. Swenson, 2nd ed. rev. by Howard Hong (Princeton, NJ: Princeton University Press, 1962); and *Concluding Unscientific Postscript* translated by David F. Swenson and Walter Lowrie

(Princeton, NJ: Princeton University Press, 1941).

25.Cf. Kierkegaard, *Either/Or*, I, 279-296.

26.Cf. *Ibid.*, II, 5-157.

27.Cf. Kierkegaard, *Fear and Trembling* and *The Sickness Unto Death*, 26-132.

28.Cf. Carl E. Krieg, *What to Believe?* (Philadelphia: Fortress Press, 1974), 6-9. Krieg points out the major problems of each view while opting for the position of "modified absolutism."

29.No more harsh and condemnatory words of Jesus are found in the gospels of the New Testament than those addressed against religious hypocrites. Cf. Mt. 23:1-33.

Chapter 5

The Christian Church

In general, Christians believe that Jesus, while on earth, wished to continue his teachings after his death by founding what has subsequently become known as the church. The English word, church, comes from the original Greek word, *ekklesia,* via the Latin, *ecclesia,* and the German, *Kirche.* The word's original root meaning seems to imply a congregation, a group of people who have been called together.[1] The Greek term, *ekklesia*, is only found twice in the New Testament Gospel accounts.[2] And many scholars of ecclesiology seem to agree that the New Testament *ekklesia* takes over and continues the meaning found in the Old Testament for *qahal Yahweh*, the community of God.[3] In the Septuagint the word, *ekklesia*, is used many times and is almost always a translation of the Hebrew, *qahal*, meaning a meeting of people having been summoned together. In the Acts of the Apostles and the Letters of St. Paul, the Greek term, *ekklesia*, is clearly used to refer to those followers of Christ who have been gathered together by God.[4] Therefore, the most common expression used today to represent the church, especially in line with its biblical root meaning encompassing both the Old and the New Testaments, is the People of God.[5] This expression refers to the Christian belief that each member of the church has been invited by God to believe in him and in his son, Jesus Christ, and to accept what Jesus has done for humankind. The invitation itself is a free gift of God mediated by the Holy Spirit.

A. The Church and the Holy Spirit

Whereas Christians generally believe that the church was called into existence by the revelation of God in Jesus Christ, so too they also believe that it is sustained by the Holy Spirit. Therefore, the real unity of the church is invisible. When St. Paul asserts that: "No one can say 'Jesus is Lord' except by the Holy Spirit" (1 Cor. 12:3), he is indicating that the Holy Spirit is responsible for creating and calling together the People of God into the church. Jesus indicated that the Holy Spirit would guide his followers "into all the truth" (Jn. 16:13) after being the efficient cause of their spiritual regeneration.[6] This same Spirit operates when and where it wills, meaning that the Holy Spirit is at work both within and outside the church itself.[7] Therefore, the church itself cannot dictate to the Spirit; it can only ask and pray to it. The church is not the Spirit, but the Spirit is the dynamic power of God behind the church, which is made up of sinners who have received justification. The Spirit not only acts upon the church as a whole, but also upon individual Christians. There are a variety of gifts or charisms of the Spirit which work together for the common good of all.[8]

With regard to the operation of the Holy Spirit upon individual members of the church, there have been two rather extreme views espoused in Christian church history. One view tended to place the entire stress on the power of the Holy Spirit as the sole source for people doing anything at all good in terms of living the Christian life. This view, at the same time, maintained a person's utter depravity and sinfulness in the sight of God.[9] Conclusions that came about from this understanding of the Holy Spirit's action upon people led to beliefs in predestination, irresistible grace, indefectible perseverance, and a kind of determinism in general. Another opposite, extreme view claimed that people are totally responsible for all of their decisions in life. People work out their own salvation literally by the performance of good works without any outside help. This more Pelagian[10] view of human beings and salvation minimizes the operation of the Holy Spirit within the church and upon the individual Christian. A more moderate, middle view most Christians seem to profess regarding the action of the Holy Spirit upon human beings opts for holding to the divine initiative in the process of people's salvation, which includes the active operation of the Holy Spirit upon them. The Gospel of St. John quotes Jesus as saying: "No one can come to me unless the Father who sent me draws him" (Jn. 6:44), and: "Unless one is born of water and the Spirit, he cannot enter the kingdom of God" (Jn. 3 :5). Therefore, this view primarily sees entrance into the People of God as a gift given by God, executed by the Holy Spirit. However, this middle position also seeks to safeguard people's freedom and teaches that they can either accept or reject this gift. The task of acceptance includes making a voluntary commitment of faith expressed by living the Christian life in the church. As St. Paul commanded the Christians at Philippi: "Work out your own salvation with fear and trembling; for God is at work in you, both to will and to work for his good pleasure" (Phil. 2:12-13).

The New Testament also speaks of the fellowship of the Spirit or participation in the Spirit.[11] In this respect, each person in the church not only has an individual, vertical, and direct relationship with God through the Spirit, but also a communal, horizontal, and indirect relationship with his or her fellow human beings as well. Indeed, there really can be no genuine salvation for an individual person separate from the community of faith itself. This community of faith is the community of the Spirit. It is the Holy Spirit who is energizing, guiding, and unifying the members. Since that first Christian Pentecost,[12] the Holy Spirit has been active in the world, continuing the work of Jesus Christ through the members of his church. This work, as was noted earlier, is basically the work of reconciliation.

B. The Necessity of the Church

In recent years, with the upheaval within many traditionally cherished institutions, the Christian church has also come under careful scrutiny as an institution. Some Christians have broken away from traditional ecclesial structures and have become anonymous Christians by practicing the Christian ethic apart from belonging to an established church. In this respect, they reflect the nineteenth century father of modern existentialism, Søren Kierkegaard, who claimed that: "It is easier to become a Christian when I am not a Christian than to become a Christian when I am one."[13] Problems with institutionalized Christianity have been characteristic of many periods of the church's history.

According to traditional Roman Catholic theology dating from the thirteenth century, the pope at Rome constitutes the vicar of Jesus Christ on earth and he, with his bishops, acts in place of Christ for his church.[14] The pope himself occupies a position of primacy within the jurisdictional composition of the body of bishops. The institutional church constitutes the pilgrim people of God led by the successors of the apostles, the pope and bishops, pressing on to make Jesus Christ and his work known in the world until he returns.[15] What underlines this view of the church is the belief in apostolic succession, which is characteristic of the episcopal type churches, such as the Roman Catholic, Eastern Orthodox, and Anglican/Episcopal Churches. These churches believe that their leaders, the bishops, have authority to lead all other Christians by virtue of being the ordained successors of the original apostles themselves. This belief is based upon an interpretation of the words of the risen Jesus addressed to the eleven apostles:

> All authority in heaven and on earth has been given to me. Go therefore and make disciples of all nations, baptizing them in the name of the Father and of the Son and of the Holy Spirit, teaching them to observe all that I have commanded you; and lo, I am with you always, to the close of the age. (Mt. 28:18-20)

The belief in the primacy of jurisdiction in the church attached to the pope is based upon a reading of certain New Testament texts by Roman Catholics.[16]

Protestant, non-episcopal Christian churches, on the other hand, interpret these biblical words differently. Arguing that the above references from Matthew and John were addressed by Jesus to all of his believing disciples, they claim that the basic reality of the church is the fellowship of human beings, who live together in faith and love. In this sense, the institution is merely a structure used to facilitate fellowship. This institution can be governed either by the presbyterian form of leadership in the person of elected leaders or by the congregational form, whereby each congregation is autonomous and can choose to govern itself as it desires. The members of these churches claim that they possess the authentic apostolic teaching, especially as it is taught in the pages of the Bible. As a matter of fact, they will claim that it is possible to have apostolic succession and be entirely outside of the apostolic teaching tradition itself. Of course, the episcopal churches deny this and claim that it is their apostolic succession which guarantees the authentic apostolic teaching. And the debate has gone on especially since the time of the Protestant Reformation during the sixteenth century.

Following from their understanding of the institutional church, episcopal and non-episcopal type churches regard their ordained ministry differently. For example, in episcopal type churches an ordained bishop or priest is regarded as being qualitatively different from the rest of the church members insofar as ordination has brought about a change in the person's very being. Consequently, once a person is ordained a priest, that person is always regarded as a priest, whether or not he or she is active in that Christian community. Non-episcopal type churches, on the other hand, look at ordination as bringing about merely a change in a person's function in the Christian community. A minister is qualitatively no different from anyone else. Each Christian is a priest insofar as that person mediates Christ to others. A person is ordained principally to minister to a particular congregation by preaching the Word of God and administering the sacraments.

To answer the question of why the institutional church is needed is to be reminded of the importance and necessity of institutions in general. Usually institutions exist to fulfill certain needs, not just for today but for generations to come. The institutional church has existed in one form or another since the time of Jesus Christ. The basic beliefs of the followers of Jesus have been passed along throughout the centuries via the medium of the institutional church. Problems have arisen especially in that history when the institution has, at times, turned inward and existed for its own sake instead of for the purpose that it was intended by Jesus, to call human beings to salvation. While describing this mission of the institutionalized church, Christian theologians have delineated three, and sometimes four, major purposes that the church has for existing in the world.

The first major purpose, which is generally characterized by the Greek word, *kerygma*, is to preach the Word of God, especially the good news of the Gospel of Jesus Christ. The *kerygma* refers to the essence of the gospel itself, namely, that the Son of God became human, suffered and died for all human beings' sins, was raised from the dead, and made it possible for people to achieve the God given goal of their existence itself, friendly union with their creator. Therefore, it is incumbent upon the church to make this known to all people. As St. Paul wrote to the Romans:

> For, "every one who calls upon the name of the Lord will be saved." But how are men to call upon him in whom they have not believed? And how are they to believe in him of whom they have never heard? And how are they to hear without a preacher? And how can men preach unless they are sent? As it is written, "How beautiful are the feet of those who preach good news!" (Rom. 10:13-15)

The church then has the responsibility in every age to proclaim this good news of salvation and this is what has inspired missionary efforts of the church throughout its history.

The second major reason why the church as an institution needs to exist is to provoke Christian fellowship, support, and community. This aspect of the church's mission is generally taught in terms of the Greek word, *koinonia*. Without the mutual support of Christian believers, individual Christians would easily become disheartened and fall away from the faith itself. Operating in the realm of faith requires frequent nourishment in the form of supportive affirmation from like believers. This is one of the reasons that individual churches have periodic meetings of their members, to help the members themselves develop a genuine sense of Christian community and belonging. The mutual support that comes about at these meetings helps the believer while living the Christian life in the world at large. The criticism that some Christian denominations do not offer much of a perception of fellowship or community in the context of their worship services seems to be valid in the light of the recognition that indeed this is one of the principal reasons for the existence of the church itself.

A third major mission for the church has been described in terms of the Greek word, *diakonia*. This means that the church exists for the purpose of service to the world at large. Anthropologists teach that human beings have a social and a biological need to help others. The basis of the Christian ethic is love and this love is especially to be given in terms of service to humankind. In different churches, the form of service that is given takes various shapes, both materially and spiritually. As a matter of fact, those who hold positions of authority in the church itself view their authority in terms of service and not in terms of domination. For example, a traditional title ascribed to the pope in the Roman Catholic Church has been the Latin designation, *servus servorum Dei*, meaning "the servant of the servants of God."

Sometimes a fourth reason is given for the necessity of the church's existence and it is described by either of two Greek terms, *eucharistia* or *leitourgia*.[17] Literally, *eucharistia* means "thanksgiving". But as it is used here it refers to the Christian sacrament of Communion instituted by Jesus during his Last Supper before his arrest and subsequent death. *Leitourgia* means "liturgy" or "worship". This fourth mission for the church implies that the church also exists to worship God. This worship takes many different forms but includes the celebration of the sacraments, especially the sacrament of Holy Communion, the Lord's Supper, or the Holy Eucharist. Through this sacrament of eating and drinking together Christians generally believe that they are made holy. They profess that they have provoked a special union with Jesus Christ either in terms of a remembrance, memorial, or his real or spiritual presence, depending upon the understanding of the sacrament taken by the individual Christian congregation. Especially in terms of this thanksgiving banquet is Christian fellowship and love to be experienced in the community itself. The argument concludes that without the institutionalized church, none of the above major reasons for the existence of the church could be realized from age to age. However, Christians are not in agreement with regard to the amount and kind of organization that is needed to guarantee these goals.

C. Who is a Christian?

This question is not a very easy question to answer since there are so many different definitions that are attached to the Christian in the contemporary world. In general though, all responses to this question can be summarized into two major positions which can be called explicit and implicit. The explicit Christian is the person who has undergone some sort of conversion experience and has explicitly chosen the Christian belief system and its professed way of life. The implicit Christian would include the person who lives his or her life according to general Christian beliefs and practices, but is not aware of any conversion experience, nor even of the explicit Christian creed. Some explicit Christians will not admit that implicit faith makes a person a Christian. Other Christians admit that either explicit or implicit faith can be the mark of a Christian.

One who is a follower of Jesus Christ is generally called a Christian. Can a person who is not an explicit follower of Jesus achieve salvation? Can there be salvation without explicit conversion? What of those people who have never heard of Jesus Christ and his teachings? Can they be saved? How explicit must a person's faith be, if only explicit faith suffices for salvation? Is it possible to know and have the assurance, beyond all doubt, that one is saved? What really constitutes true, authentic faith? These and other similar questions have troubled Christians dealing with the basic question concerning who is a Christian. All Christians admit that a Christian is indeed one who follows the teachings of Jesus Christ, but the extent and precision that this implies varies greatly among Christians themselves.

D. The Unity of the Church

What has been referred to as the scandal of Christianity is the fact that there have been major differences and divisions among Christians throughout the history of Christianity. Although the Christian Nicene Creed professes to believe in "one, holy, catholic, and apostolic church,"[18] anything but a united church has been the situation among Christians for many centuries. Whereas the church created by the action of the Holy Spirit is invisible, the people of God who comprise the church itself are indeed quite visible. Lack of union in the church was apparent even in the time of the New Testament with false teachers and prophets.[19] However, the words of Jesus in the New Testament show that he himself desired a unified body of his followers: "I do not pray for these only, but also for those who believe in me through their word, that they may all be one; even as thou, Father, art in me" (Jn. 17:20-21).

The first major division within the Christian church took place in 1054 with the East-West schism, whereby the Pope in Rome and the Patriarch of Constantinople mutually excommunicated one another and their followers. Church historians tell us that this rift between the eastern and the western parts of the Christian church came about because of a number of factors, including not only religious disagreements, but also political, geographical, cultural, and linguistic differences as well. For example, was the center of Christianity in the Roman Empire to be located in the East's Constantinople (modern day Istanbul) or in the West's Rome? Who was to be head of the church, the pope of Rome or the patriarch of Constantinople? Was Greek or Latin to be the official language of the church? The doctrinal differences between the two major segments of Christianity recede into the background when one studies about the other causes of the schism.[20] The Eastern Orthodox Churches and the Roman Catholic Church still persevere in their division from one another today, even though the 1968 gesture of removing the mutual excommunications by Pope Paul VI and Patriarch Athanagoras IV has helped to make relations between the churches more amicable than in former times.

The third major segment of the Christian churches comprises the Protestant churches. The sixteenth century brought about a further splintering of the church in the West with the attempt by some of its members to reform it from its corrupt beliefs and practices. These protestors did not originally intend to break away from the existing Roman Church, only to reform it. However, as things worked out, further divisions, antagonisms, and even hostilities broke out among Christians in the West with the corresponding proliferation of churches. As was indicated earlier, there are nearly two hundred different Christian denominations and churches in North America alone. All of these denominations, however, can be seen to derive their origins from one or the other of four basic branches found in Protestantism today. There are those churches that are Lutheran[21] in origin and orientation. Secondly, there are the Reformed and Presbyterian denominations that have followed and interpreted especially the teachings of John Calvin.[22] Thirdly, there are all those who basically follow the radical Protestant reformers in the sixteenth century called the Anabaptists.[23] The final group derive their beliefs and teachings essentially from the Anglican Church.[24] The Anglican Church has been referred to as the "bridge church" because it more closely resembles the Roman Catholic Church than any of the other Protestant churches.

To speak of the unity of the church does not mean to imply that unity is the same as uniformity. The experience of religion in the United States of America has probably taught the world that perhaps the more constructive approach to the subject is where there is permitted great diversity. This fact, of course, is guaranteed by the Constitution of the United States where one is free to believe or not to believe as one chooses. Perhaps a case could be made for this concept of diversity in unity by appealing to the words of Jesus: "In my Father's house are many rooms" (Jn. 14:2). The twentieth century has brought about concerted attempts by Christians to emphasize the unity that the different Christian churches do possess and to play down the animosities of the past that have all too often characterized the various churches' relationships. This movement to reunify the Church of Jesus Christ has been called ecumenism[25] and by extension the term applies to all people of good will who attempt to provoke more amicable relationships between Christians and other religious believers and even non-believers. Truly there are differences that distinguish, rather than separate, the Christian churches. Christians are united in their belief that Jesus is the Messiah and that he has called human beings to salvation. With this has come about a renewed interest in the study of the Bible and especially the Gospel of Jesus Christ, realizing that indeed this is the standard or norm for unity. The age of ecumenism is an exciting one for Christians insofar as they are actively seeking to bring about Christian unity in a divided church and the concord of all people of integrity and good will.

E. The Church and the Kingdom of God

The words "kingdom of God" are found about a hundred times in the synoptic gospel accounts of the New Testament.[26] For example, near the beginning of St. Mark's account of the gospel, he quotes Jesus as saying: "The time is fulfilled, and the kingdom of God is at hand; repent, and believe in the gospel" (Mk. 1:15). According to a study done by Professor Hans Küng,[27] exegetical and theological interpretations of this reign of God share the following notions: 1) The kingdom is an eschatological reality, meaning the definitive and full reign of God at the end of time and which is now "at hand." 2) The reign of God is brought about by God himself and not by human beings. 3) The reign of God is not a material, but a spiritual or religious kingdom. 4) The reign of God is a bringing about of salvation for sinners, rather than their condemnation. 5) And the reign of God demands a radical decision on the part of human beings for God, involving repentance for sin.

The kingdom of God, however, is not usually identified with the church itself.[28] The church, which consists of sinners and shares much of the world's ambiguity, cannot be regarded as the reign of God in his kingdom. The church itself continually prays for the realization of the kingdom of God with the words from the Lord's Prayer, "thy kingdom come" (Mt. 6:10). Whereas, according to Christian belief, the risen Christ is reigning in his church, the reigning of God in his kingdom implies the definitive and full manifestation of God's holiness at the end of time. At present, this is seen only through faith in an ambiguous and sinful world.

Beyond the very general assertions mentioned above, New Testament scholars are divided as to the meaning and use of the expression, kingdom of God, in the preaching of Jesus. In general, at least four basically different views of eschatology can be found taught among Christians. Eschatology is the study of the last things and it refers to that part of Christian beliefs that deals with the final end or goal of human beings. In this instance, however, the various eschatological views regarding the kingdom of God will be studied.

One view, proposed by such scholars as Albert Schweitzer,[29] claims that the preaching of Jesus about the kingdom of God was thoroughly influenced by Jewish apocalypticism. This apocalypticism, or attempt to reveal the future, was centered about the restoration of the covenant with Israel and God's reign over the entire world. Therefore, the teachings of Jesus contained a certain imminence to them. For example, the gospel words: "The kingdom of God is at hand" (Mk. 1:15) ring with a sense of imminence and urgency. This view claims that Jesus looked for the end of the world and the definitive and full establishment of the kingdom within his own lifetime. Of course, this theory is also founded upon the belief that Jesus the man was not in possession of his divine omniscience during his life on earth, based upon the kenotic theory.[30] However, Schweitzer and his followers go on to assert the theory that Jesus and the first Christians' belief about the end of history occurring in their own generation has been nullified by the fact of the ongoingness of history. Therefore, the kingdom lies wholly in the future and so this view has come to be known as consistent, futurist, or thoroughgoing eschatology.

A second view of the kingdom of God is called proleptic or realized eschatology and it was proposed by C. H. Dodd.[31] This view claims that the kingdom of God was fully realized with the coming of Jesus Christ. For example, Dodd literally takes to be true the words of Jesus: "The kingdom of God has come upon you" (Mt. 12:28).[32] However, the resurrection of Jesus, the descent of the Holy Spirit, and the missionary history of the church are not to be excluded as factors in the coming of the kingdom, since they all follow from the kingdom being present. The futuristic references about the kingdom are explained away as reflecting the beliefs of the primitive Christian community, and not those of Jesus. [33] The second coming of Jesus will pronounce the absolute or sheer finality of the kingdom itself, which already has been realized.[34]

A third view can be called salvation history or self-realizing eschatology. Both Roman Catholic and Protestant biblical scholars hold to this view, especially the Roman Catholic, Rudolf Schnackenburg,[35] and the Protestant, Oscar Cullmann.[36] This view tends to combine the present and the future elements in the teaching of Jesus about the kingdom of God. The kingdom of God became present with the coming of Jesus, but is still awaiting its fulfillment. There is then a tension existing between the already present and the not yet fulfilled aspects of the kingdom in the drama of the history of salvation. Cullmann, for example, looks at history as consisting of a straight line running between the moment of creation and the return of Jesus at the end of time, the *parousia*. This line has been intersected at its midpoint by the coming of Jesus Christ. The decisive battle has already occurred and has been won by Jesus as the belief in the resurrection teaches. However, the important mopping-up exercises must still go on after this major battle and victory until the day of total victory, which will take place at Jesus' return.[37] Therefore, the kingdom is indeed already present, but not in its fulness and completeness until the *parousia*.

Existentialist eschatology constitutes a fourth view about the kingdom of God. The major proponent of this view was Rudolf Bultmann.[38] This view teaches that any moment or situation in which one has to make an ultimately significant decision is eschatological. This involves both a moment of challenge and a deliberate decision of commitment to God. It does not lie in the future, but rather is the time God gives to each person as an opportunity for making ultimately significant decisions. This view attempts to convert both the past and the future into the present moment as being of supreme importance for the realization of the kingdom. The biblical images concerning a future event in this regard need to be demythologized. For example, eternal life is the life one receives now; judgment is the crisis in which one now stands; and the end-time itself is the present moment of challenge[39] in which the issue of life and death is being decided. Therefore, one's existence in faith is an eschatological event, making the kingdom of God present.

And so the theological discussion goes on within the Christian community over the teaching of Jesus about the kingdom. Whether the kingdom already is in existence and to what extent it exists, if it exists, remains a matter of interpretation of the New Testament words: "The kingdom of God is at hand" (Mk. 1:15). The pilgrim church of Jesus Christ, comprising God's own people, will continue to debate over this and other issues of belief in the future. They will study these problems with a sense of unity with one another, as they look forward to the *parousia* itself. The one, holy, catholic, and apostolic church does have the promise of the resurrected Jesus himself that he will remain with his church until the end of time.[40]

Notes -Chapter 5

1.Cf. Hans Küng, *The Church* (NY: Sheed and Ward, 1967), 79-87.

2.Cf. Mt. 16:18; 18:17.

3.Cf. Küng, *The Church*, 81-83.

4.Cf. *Ibid.*, 83-84.

5.Cf. 1 Pet. 2:9; Gal. 6:16.

6.Cf. Jn. 3:3-8.

7.Cf. 1 Cor. 12:4-31.

8.Cf. 1 Cor.. 12:4-31.

9.For example, John Calvin wrote that: "Man is so enslaved by sin, as to be of his own nature incapable of an effort, or even an inspiration, towards that which is good." Cf. J. Calvin, *op. cit.*, 51.

10.Pelagianism, a heresy condemned by the Council of Orange in 529, essentially maintained that people are fully responsible for their own individual actions and do not absolutely need God's special help or grace. St. Augustine especially fought against this belief while teaching the traditional, biological transmission theory of Original Sin. Cf. J. H. Leith, *op. cit.*, 37-45.

11.Cf.,e.g., 2 Cor. 13:14; Phil. 2:1.

12.Cf. Acts 2:1-13.

13.Kierkegaard, *Concluding Unscientific Postscript*, 327.

14.Cf. Walter M. Abbot, ed., "Dogmatic Constitution on the Church," *The Documents of Vatican II* (NY: America Press, 1966), 37-56.

15.Ibid., 24.

16.Cf. especially Mt. 16:13-20 and Jn. 21:15-17.

17.Cf., e.g., Bruce D. Marshall's "Why Bother with the Church?" *The Christian Century* (Jan. 24, 1996), pp. 74-76.

18.Leith, *op. cit.*, 33.

19.Cf. Mt. 7:15, 24:24; 2 Cor.. 11:13; Gal. 2:4; 1 Jn. 4:1; etc.

20.A good historical survey of these differences can be found in Philip Schaff, *History of the Christian Church*, IV (NY: Chas. Scribner's Sons, 1910), 304-320.

21.Martin Luther (1483-1546) was German theologian and religious reformer.

22.John Calvin (1509-1564) was a Swiss theologian and religious reformer.

23.The Anabaptist Protestant reformers insisted that baptism was for adult believers only and baptism was to be performed by the total immersion in water of the person to be baptized.

24.The Anglican Church came about after the King of England, Henry VIII (1509-1547), broke relations with Rome and made himself head of the Church of England.

25.The ecumenical movement was begun by the Protestant churches in the early part of the twentieth century and the Roman Catholic Church entered this movement with its "Decree on Ecumenism" at the Second Vatican Council in 1964. The word "ecumenical" is from the Greek word "*oikoumene*" and means the inhabited earth. Cf. Acts 17:7; Mt. 24:14; and Heb. 2:5.

26.Cf. Küng, *The Church*, 43.

27.Cf. *ibid.*, 47-54.

28.Cf. *ibid.*, 88-96.

29.Cf. Schweitzer, *op. cit.*, 221-269; 330-403.

30.The kenotic theory was already discussed in Chapter 2 of this work.

31.Cf. C. H. Dodd, *The Apostolic Preaching and its Developments* (NY: Harper's 1962), 79-96.

32.Other New Testament references cited by Dodd are: Acts 2:16; 2 Cor. 3:18; 5:17; Col. 1:13; Tit. 3:5; Heb. 6:5; 1 Pet. 1:23; and 1 Jn. 2:8.

33.Cf. Dodd, *op. cit.*, 36-41.

34.Cf. *ibid.*, 93.

35.Cf. Rudolf Schnackenburg, *God's Rule and Kingdom* (Edinburgh-London: Nelson, 1963).

36.Cf. Oscar Cullmann, *Christ and Time* (Philadelphia: The Westminster Press, 1964).

37.Cf. *ibid.*, 121-174.

38.Cf. Rudolf Bultmann, *Primitive Christianity in Its Contemporary Setting* (Cleveland: The World Publishing Co., 1969), 86-93 and Rudolf Bultmann, *Theology of the New Testament, I* (NY: Chas. Scribner's Sons, 1951), 4-11.

39.The Greek term, *kairos*, is used by some theologians to distinguish between chronological, measurable time, denoted by the Greek term, *chronos*, and the special moments of decision in people's lives called *kairos* situations. Cf. Eph. 5:16 which refers to the "time" that a person should make the most of, signifying the right opportunity, special moment, or right time. That which has been named "crisis theology" emphasizes that each human being continually lives in a time of opportunity, crisis, and judgment.

40.Cf. Mt. 28:20.

Chapter 6

Christian Ethics

Christian ethics and morality follow from what Christians believe about God, themselves, other people, and the world. Because of certain beliefs, Christians act in a specified way while living their lives in the world. At times, this area of study is referred to as moral theology, to distinguish it from dogmatic or systematic theology which deals with creedal beliefs. However, to profess a specific ethic or to follow certain moral standards presupposes that people have the capacity to make choices in that regard. This follows from the Christian view of human beings.

A. The Christian View of Human Beings

Christians believe that human beings are wholly different from all of God's other creation.[1] Besides sharing physical and perhaps even psychological characteristics with other created beings, Christians believe that human beings are also spiritual entities.[2] By this they mean that they not only have in common many things that other living beings possess, especially animals, such as bodies that need air, nourishment, shelter, rest, and so on, and even mental capacities, but human beings are also entities who are conscious and aware of themselves and can love. They can literally step back and look at themselves reflectively. They have a memory that reminds them of the past and an imagination that can take them into the future. They can thus transcend both time and place. Furthermore, human beings can love and, in fact, need love to survive. To be able to love, made to the image and likeness of God as the Bible describes them, presupposes that human beings are free.[3]

The Christian view of human beings, however, does not advance the belief that people are completely free. In general, Christians admit that a person's freedom is definitely qualified by biological, psychological, and sociological factors.[4] People are, to a certain extent, determined as well as free. But without freedom, ethics and morality are not possible, and without morality, no human life is possible. Essentially then, ethics or moral standards are norms to help guide people in living their freedom. There are several religious moralities prevalent in the world today. The points of convergence among these various moralities are much more numerous and fundamental than the points of divergence.[5] Also these religious moralities usually appeal to generosity and altruism, striving to keep harmonious relations among human beings.

The Christian view of human beings as physical, psychological, and spiritual beings sees them existing in a rather ambiguous fashion.[6] Not only does the Christian see himself or herself as both free and determined, but also, for example, as an individual existing in a community. This means that people not only have responsibilities to themselves as individual persons, but they also have certain social responsibilities to their fellow human beings. It is not a question of either/or, but one of both/and. This tension within the human being is the source of much consternation in given circumstances and each person is called to make his or her own decisions within the framework of the guidelines found in the Christian tradition. These and other polarities exist within human beings and make it difficult to give an adequate description of them beyond broad categories. However, within the context of the exercise of one's freedom, a person is responsible for his or her own decisions. To act irresponsibly is to fall into what Christians call "sin."

B. Sin in Christian Tradition

The concept of Original Sin was already examined in chapter three. Here the concern is with personal or actual sin. Sin involves a turning away from God and what God has made known he wants human beings to do, and a turning toward a creature.[7] In more contemporary times sin has been defined as the violation of a loving relationship one has with God and with one's fellow human being.[8] The biblical notion of sin also always views sin as a violation of a relationship.[9] In addition, sin involves a refusal on the part of a person to be the human being that God wants that person to be. By deliberately choosing to go against God's will in this regard, a person violates his or her relationship with God.[10] A person, therefore, by sinning is guilty too of an injustice to God, who is one's

Lord and Master.[11] The sinner also has pulled himself or herself down insofar as he or she is not the person he or she was intended to be or could be. By sinning, a person has alienated other people as well, those who depend upon humans living their existences as God intended.[12] Even the earth suffers when a person sins because of the sinner's irresponsibility to the earth over which God has put human beings in charge.[13] Indeed, when a person sins, there are many ramifications of that sin.

Christians vary in their understanding with regard to the degree of sinfulness incurred by the sinner. In basic Protestant thought, a sin is a sin and there are no varying degrees of sinfulness. Roman Catholic teaching, however, distinguishes between mortal and venial sins.[14] The former are serious and result in severing one's loving relationship with God. The latter, however, are less serious and only weaken, but do not destroy, that relationship. Using an analogy from the legal profession, it is somewhat like the difference between a felony and a misdemeanor. For a sin to be mortal, a serious or grave matter must be involved, there must be full advertence or reflection concerning the seriousness of the intended sin, and there must be the full and free consent of the sinner to the sin itself. If any one of these conditions is missing, there is no mortal sin, but at the most, only venial sin. Based upon this distinction, it follows that unrepentant mortal sins will merit eternal damnation at death, whereas unforgiven venial sins can be made up for by suffering even after death. This suffering after death will take place in a state called Purgatory, which will be discussed in chapter seven. According to Protestant Christians, Purgatory does not exist and so all unrepentant sin is equally condemned in the eyes of God.

Christians also recognize that human beings must contend with certain temptations to sin that come to them from various sources.[15] One of the major sources of temptation to sin has been traditionally recognized by Christians to be the Devil or Satan. As was seen earlier, while investigating the life of Jesus on earth, Jesus himself underwent and survived a triple temptation from Satan at the beginning of his public life.[16] Another major source of temptation to sin arises from within human beings themselves. Traditionally, this has been referred to as concupiscence or desires of the flesh.[17] Although at times Christians have tended to equate concupiscence only with sexual allurements, this temptation to sin refers to any inclination arising from within a person tempting that person to misuse personal freedom and to sin. A third major source of temptation to sin has been defined in terms of evil in the world.[18] Depending upon how one views the Christian concept of

Original Sin, the world is either fallen through the sin of Adam and Eve or there is merely sin in the world into which each person is born and must contend. This fallen world or evil in the world continually presents a person with temptations to participate in its basic sinfulness. Nevertheless, although Christians believe that each person is definitely a sinner, they also believe that God gives to people the necessary help or grace to overcome temptations to sin.[19] Whether people avail themselves of this help is another matter. Temptations to sin are not sins of themselves, but they can, and do indeed, lead people into sin. Therefore, Christians usually reason that they should not unnecessarily and willfully place themselves in situations that they know will provoke temptation to sin.

Many Christians also distinguish between sins of omission and commission. Sins of commission refer to those sins whereby a person deliberately acts in a certain way as to violate his or her loving relationship with God and his or her fellow human beings. These sins involve a positive action on the part of people to violate God's will for them. Sins of omission, on the other hand, refer to the disregard of one's obligations as a Christian whereby one neglects to do the good that one knows one must do in response to one's Christian vocation. The New Testament parable of the sheep and the goats indicts those people guilty of sins of omission with the words of Jesus: "Truly, I say to you, as you did it not to one of the least of these, you did it not to me" (Mt. 25:45). Some Christians in contemporary times feel that these sins of omission are the greater and more numerous sins to be found in the present age, although moral systems traditionally have been quite sensitive to the evil done by sins of omission.[20] While reflecting upon sins of omission, Pastor Martin Niemöller, a survivor of the concentration camp at Dachau, Germany during World War II, was quoted after the war as saying:

> First they came for the communists, but I was not a communist---so I said nothing. They came for the social democrats, but I was not a social democrat---so I did nothing. Then came the trade unionists, but I was not a trade unionist. And then they came for the Jews, but I was not a Jew---so I did little. Then when they came for me, there was no one left who could stand up for me.[21]

What Niemöller experienced, a remark attributed to Edmund Burke many years earlier affirmed that: "All that is necessary for evil to triumph is for good men to do nothing."[22]

Another distinction that is oftentimes found among Christians with regard to sin is the difference between sins of the heart and sins of action. Sins of the heart are internal sins and they arise in a person's evil disposition or intention, whether or not the person is capable of acting upon the evil desire. Jesus' words regarding adultery have been the subject of much discussion among Christians who distinguish sins of the heart: "You have heard that it was said, 'You shall not commit adultery.' But I say to you that every one who looks at a woman lustfully has already committed adultery with her in his heart" (Mt. 5:27-28). Indeed, all sins are sins of the heart, but not all sins of the heart are sins of action. Sins of action are external sins where there is not only the intention or desire to sin, but this desire is positively acted upon. Some Christians, therefore, maintain that sins of action are more serious than merely sins of the heart. Again, all sin has an inward character to it. One cannot commit sin if one does not deliberately will to do it. The ability to choose is essential to the Christian concept of sin. That is one of the reasons why Christians cannot accept a current definition of the human person as merely a conditioned reflex.[23]

According to Christian tradition, there have been listed seven major sources of sin called either the seven capital sins, the seven deadly sins, or the seven cardinal sins. In St. John's first letter in the New Testament he wrote that: "For all that is in the world, the lust of the flesh and the lust of the eyes and the pride of life, is not of the Father but is of the world" (1 Jn. 2:16). The writer of this letter attempted to make the point that there are indeed temptations to sin in the world, but he went on to state that: "The world passes away, and the lust of it; but he who does the will of God abides for ever" (1 Jn. 2: 17). From about the fifth century, Christians have expanded this list of sources of sin to seven, which is the biblical number designating fullness or completion.[24] These seven are pride, covetousness, lust, intemperance, envy, anger, and sloth.[25]

The capital sin of pride or vainglory denotes that source of sin that views a person as self-sufficient. One is so preoccupied with oneself as to forget about God. St. Paul wrote to the Romans: "Claiming to be wise, they became fools, and exchanged the glory of the immortal God for images resembling mortal man...." (Rom. 1:22-23). Pride is the vice opposed to the virtue of humility. Whereas humility deals with a correct and truthful attitude towards oneself, especially in one's relationship with God, pride involves a false estimate of one's worth and dignity. Many claim that pride is the basic sin insofar as a person is setting himself or herself up as an idol in place of God, the creator and sustainer of all. The proud person views himself or herself as his or her own first beginning and last end and does not recognize his or her continual dependence upon God. Jesus himself praised humility and condemned pride with the words: "Whoever exalts himself will be humbled, and whoever humbles himself will be exalted" (Mt. 23:12). Some Christians have misunderstood the meaning of the word humility and have equated it with humiliation. Humility is simply truth about oneself, and proud individuals refuse to recognize the truth about themselves in their relationship with God and others.

Covetousness or avarice is that source of sin that is connected with the inordinate pursuit of material things. The avaricious person is the greedy person who is continually attempting to acquire wealth and material things to the exclusion of spiritual things. This person is also inclined to see earthly goods as the only and final goal of human existence to the extent that he or she ends up idolizing material things by completely indulging himself or herself in them. Moved by one's craving for material things for oneself, one has little if any regard for the needs of one's fellow human beings. Yet Jesus is quoted as having said:

> Do not lay up for yourselves treasures on earth, where moth and rust consume and where thieves break in and steal, but lay up for yourselves treasures in heaven, where neither moth nor rust consumes and where thieves do not break in and steal. For where your treasure is, there will your heart be also. (Mt. 6:19-21)

Elsewhere, Jesus puts it even more clearly:

> No servant can serve two masters; for either he will hate the one and love the other, or he will be devoted to the one and despise the other. You cannot serve God and mammon (Lk. 16:13).[26]

Therefore, Christians believe that a certain renunciation of material things is demanded by those who are attempting to follow Jesus. The extent of this renunciation involves a matter of priorities for living one's Christian life.

The capital sin of lust refers to the excessive craving for sexual pleasures from another who has become an object to be used and enjoyed, rather than respected as a person. The lustful person is not drawn to the other by the mystery of love, but due to the selfish desires of the flesh. Lust, therefore, is the result of excessive self-love. It can even blind a person to the point where one becomes totally insensible to spiritual reality and only concentrates on one's own physical gratification. Lust has no respect for people in and of themselves, but only acknowledges them insofar as they can give the lustful person pleasure. Rather than coveting things, the lustful person covets other people for sexual pleasure alone. This source of sin oftentimes is the basis for sins of adultery and fornication. St. Paul wrote about those who lust that:

> God gave them up in the lusts of their hearts to impurity, to the dishonoring of their bodies among themselves, because they exchanged the truth about God for a lie and worshiped and served the creature rather than the Creator, who is blessed forever. (Rom. 1:24-25)[27]

Intemperance refers to the lack of moderation and restraint with regard to a person's natural appetites of hunger and thirst. Intemperance in eating is called gluttony and refers to excessive eating. St. Paul wrote about gluttons with these words: "Their end is destruction, their god is the belly, and they glory in their shame, with minds set on earthly things" (Phil. 3:19). Intemperance with reference to the drinking of alcohol is called drunkenness, intoxication, or inebriation. In this state, one is deprived of the use of one's reason and even one's moral freedom. Again, St. Paul condemned the drunkard with these words: "Do not be deceived; neither the immoral, nor idolaters, nor adulterers, nor homosexuals, nor thieves, nor the greedy, nor drunkards, nor revilers, nor robbers will inherit the kingdom of God" (1 Cor. 6:9-10). Christian ethics generally teach that all of God's creation can be enjoyed in moderation, but excesses are to be avoided. God's good creation is to be used, but not abused. This belief is expressed by the Latin theological maxim, *in medio stat virtus*, which means virtue stands in the middle between extremes. Jesus himself was vilified by his enemies because he ate and drank with sinners. He made reference to this with the words: "For John came neither eating nor drinking, and they say, 'He has a demon'; the Son of man came eating and drinking, and they say, 'Behold a glutton and a drunkard, a friend of tax collectors and sinners!'" (Mt. 11:18-19). Whereas it is true that many Christians deny themselves legitimate pleasures with regard to their natural appetites, they admit that they do this for higher motives, and especially so that they do not become a scandal or stumbling block for their neighbor.[28] Intemperance can lead to obesity and the endangering of one's health, familial degeneracy, spiritual laziness, and so on.

Envy is that capital sin that begrudges and resents a neighbor's desirable possessions or qualities. The possessions or qualities possessed by another are seen as a very real obstacle to one's own glory. Instead of admiring, complimenting, and rejoicing over the good fortune of one's neighbor, the envious person is unhappy because of the neighbor's possessions or qualities and desires them personally. The envious person is thus inclined to slander and run down the character of the person of whom he or she is envious and even rejoice when that same person experiences misfortunes in life. Ultimately, envy can lead to the hatred of others and a prevalent bitterness with respect to one's life in general because it does not possess the material goods nor the qualities that one deems are all too desirable. Needless to say, the envious person is not very content with himself or herself and the circumstances in his or her life and thus is not a very happy person. Pontius Pilate, the Roman procurator of Judea at the time of Jesus, recognized the motives of the Jewish leaders plotting against Jesus' life to be out of envy: "For he knew that it was out of envy that they had delivered him up" (Mt. 27:18).

Anger is an instinctive urge in people making them hostile to what they regard as evil. Whereas Christians admit that it can be good to become emotionally disgusted with evil and to suppress and repel whatever is hostile in that respect, they also admit that their anger can be evil as well. Justifiable anger or indignation, as some refer to this type of justifiable anger, is found in the person of Jesus himself who opposed evil in the temple at Jerusalem:

> And Jesus entered the temple of God and drove out all who sold and bought in the temple, and overturned the tables of the moneychangers and the seats of those who sold pigeons. He said to them, "It is written, 'My house shall be called a house of prayer'; but you make it a den of robbers." (Mt. 21:12-13)

When anger goes beyond right reason and is motivated by selfish concerns alone, it becomes sinful.[29] At this juncture, anger leads to quarreling, abuse of others, insults, cursing, and even physical harm to others by fighting, injury, or murder. Closely tied to anger is the fault of impatience.[30] One who is inclined to become angry at little provocation needs to develop the virtue of Christian forbearance or patience. However, again it must be recognized that evil not only needs to be repelled by Christians, but must be recognized and affirmed for what it is.

The seventh capital sin of spiritual sloth may be defined simply as spiritual laziness. The spiritually slothful or indolent person has very little regard for spiritual things and totally concentrates his or her interests and efforts upon material matters alone. This source of sin can lead a person into all sorts of sins of indulgence where worldly things can even become idols. Physical pleasures alone are sought by the slothful person to the extent that he or she can end up even hating the morally good altogether.[31]

All of these primary sources of sin are considered major vices by Christians because of the extent of their influence upon human beings. Some Christians hesitate to emphasize them to any great degree because of the danger of falling into a casuistic understanding of Christian morality rather than following an authentic, personal morality. Casuistry is the application of general moral principles to particular cases and oftentimes falls into a kind of legalistic view of ethics to the extent that it is divorced from a fundamental Christian understanding of basic beliefs. This then leads into the next section while trying to understand Christian ethics based upon the various approaches taken by Christians themselves attempting to live authentic Christian lives.

C. Different Approaches to Christian Ethics

One way of distinguishing between approaches taken by Christian ethicists or moralists is to classify them as either teleological or deontological. Teleological ethics, the word coming from the Greek *telos* meaning end or goal, attempts to define what is good and valuable for people and then proceeds to show them how they can best achieve that good end or goal. One of the most influential Christian teleological ethics was constructed by Thomas Aquinas in the thirteenth century.[32] He basically taught that people have both a natural and a supernatural goal or end. Both of these goals or ends have their own proper principles and virtues to follow to achieve them. These need to be applied in particular cases by individuals while living their Christian lives. Aquinas' influence is still felt in this regard in contemporary forms of official Roman Catholic ethical teaching.[33]

Deontological ethics, the word coming from the Greek *deo* meaning that which is binding or needful, concerns itself primarily with binding moral obligations or duties, not the end or goal of human beings as such. Whereas teleological systems are concerned with the good end informing moral choices, deontological systems are preoccupied with what a person must do regardless of the consequences. The ethics of the Protestant Reformers, which distinguished between the Law and the Gospel, pointed out people's responsibility for accepting and fulfilling God's gift and will for them by following his precepts spelled out especially in the Decalogue,[34] the Sermon on the Mount,[35] and elsewhere. Practically speaking, however, both the teleological and deontological ethical systems are relatively close positions. While defining a person's good end or goal, certain duties to be fulfilled by that person are implied; while delineating a person's duties, some understanding of the good end or goal is certainly presumed. Yet there is a difference of point of departure and, therefore, style in both systems.[36]

Christians are inclined to approach solving their individual ethical problems in different ways. Some Christians seek to find out and obey the laws gleaned from the Bible and from their church authorities. To be moral for them consists of adhering to these laws in all circumstances of life. This position is one of legalism[37] and holds sacred not only God's laws, but also all human laws promulgated by legitimate authority both within and outside the church itself. If any of these laws come into conflict with one another, the higher law is chosen over the lower law. For example, a law given by God and found in the Bible is superior to a humanly-made law. Legalistic views of ethics have come under severe attack in more recent times for one reason or another, but this approach does offer the person who follows it a confident security and certainty. Usually the legalist does not have to agonize over ethical decisions. They are made for one by someone else. But, at the same time, it is not always easy to act on someone else's conscience and obey a specific law.

The opposite of this legalistic system is the position of antinomianism[38] which suggests that there are no laws or restraints upon people. One can do anything one wants. Of course, Christian ethics abhors this ethical approach, viewing it as leading to moral anarchy.

However, there is a middle ground, so to speak, between legalism and antinomianism. This position maintains that because each person is unique and because each situation in life is also unique, no norm nor law can possibly anticipate what a person's response to a particular situation will be except the Christian law of love. Because of its insistence upon the uniqueness of each situation or the context of one's actions, this approach is frequently referred to as either situationism or contextualism.[39] Christian situationists/contextualists insist that love is the only binding obligation incumbent upon human beings. No two situations are alike. All human beings have to ask themselves what the demands of love are for them in their own unique situations in life. They have the Bible and the traditional teachings of the church to fall back upon while discovering what the exigencies of love are for them in their own circumstances. This position affirms that each person must agonize over his or her own choices, whatever they might be, in a personal relationship with God and his or her fellow human beings. It is this writer's judgment that few Christians indeed are strict situationists/contextualists or legalists. It would seem that the majority of Christians vacillate somewhere between legalism and situationism/contextualism. A major difference found while comparing these two ethical approaches is that with legalism, a good end never justifies the use of evil means. But for situationism/contextualism a good end can justify the use of evil means. With the Christian's freedom also goes the corresponding responsibility. Whatever ethical decisions are made, regardless of the approach taken, people carry with them the individual responsibility for the decisions themselves. To act irresponsibly in this regard falls into the area of sin and guilt for the Christian.

D. The Problem of Evil

Traditionally, evil has been defined in terms of negation. For example, St. Augustine referred to it as the privation or absence of good or being.[40] St. Athanasius wrote: "What is evil is not, but what is good is."[41] Therefore, good has been defined, in terms of being, as anything that would tend to promote and enhance God's creation, which when God created, was very good.[42] Evil then would be viewed as the antithesis of good insofar as it would refer to those factors in history that would tend to destroy being and deter God's good creation. However, there seems to be a vast combination of both good and evil in the world and this creates a basic question for Christian believers who profess belief in a good, omnipotent God. Why does God permit evil to exist? This problem of evil is one of the more difficult dilemmas that any religion professing belief in a good and omnipotent God must confront. As a matter of fact, this same problem of evil is at the root of much contemporary agnosticism and atheism, since there are many people who recognize this problem and, rather than hold God responsible for evil, prefer to simply not believe in or be convinced of the existence of God at all.

Most Christians, however, hold that because God chose to create human beings with freedom, he necessarily had to go along with their misusing their freedom by sinning and thereby bringing evil into the world or contributing to the evil that is already there. Some would explain the evil that innocent people have to endure as the result of punishment for their own former sins or the sins of their ancestors. Others view it as a test from God to prove their loyalty to him. Still others view evil solely in terms of Satan's influence upon creation, and those who claim that Satan's power is even greater than that of God, end up worshiping Satan himself. Some attempt to solve the problem of evil in the world by asserting that it is only accidental and is due to an imperfect creation that is still evolving toward perfection, that God limited his omnipotence when he created and has let nature take its own course.

It would seem, however, that very many Christians today follow St. Augustine's distinction between natural or physical evil and human or moral evil.[43] While admitting that evil is mysterious, which is indeed a safe position to start from, they assert that natural evil such as floods, earthquakes, famines, diseases, and the like is not really evil at all. Much of it is accidental and could have been avoided. It is mysterious, but people can do a great deal to help prevent some of it, such as building flood walls, discovering cures for diseases, predicting the occurrence and severity of earthquakes, and so on. This view does not see natural evil that befalls human beings to be in any way a punishment from God for sin. It, many times, goes on to assert that if one were able to see the all-encompassing picture God has of creation, one would see that what is referred to as evil is really not evil at all. It is only apparent evil from the human perspective. This is generally known as the tapestry theory with reference to what is called natural or physical evil. People only see specific threads and not the complete picture or tapestry as God does with his omniscience. Jesus testifies to this with his response to the question about the reason a certain man was born blind:

> And his disciples asked him, "Rabbi, who sinned, this man or his parents, that he was born blind?" Jesus answered, "It was not that this man sinned, or his parents, but that the works of God might be made manifest in him." (Jn. 9:2-3)

And Jesus then went on to open the man's eyes so that he could see.

On the other hand, there is in fact human or moral evil in the world which is a product of the abuse of human freedom. A person's sin, which violates one's relationship with God and one's fellow human beings, is the cause of human or moral evil. Whether one sins as an individual or whether one cooperates in sinning with others, one is responsible for these sins and must pay the penalty, insofar as one's sin has disrupted the moral order itself, bringing with it evil consequences not only for oneself but for others as well. It has been said that every good action of human beings uplifts the world and every sinful action tends to lower the world. No one sins in a vacuum. People are interrelated and all suffer from one person's sins. It is kind of like throwing a pebble into a pool of water and watching the ripple of waves flow away from the point of initial impact made by the small stone. For example, the human race does not become involved in wars over a single sin. It is the daily sinful actions of people that mushroom into large scale human disasters just as it is the daily attempts by people to live in loving relationships with God and one another that result in the advancement of the human race itself. Witness, for example, the efforts of people to help conquer certain diseases by the cooperation of nations through the World Health Organization and the eradication of diseases such as smallpox. Christianity believes that wars are not caused by God, but by people themselves. God could prevent these wars only by, at the same time, destroying people's freedom.

Why innocent people suffer for the sins of others has remained a problem even in Christianity. There really is no sufficient intellectual answer, but there is one in terms of faith in God. The hackneyed phrase, "God knows best," is often overused in this regard and is no different than those words of the Old Testament figure, Job, who was also perplexed by this same problem. For Job, it was sufficient for him to know by his belief that God exists and that his misfortunes are then to be counted as mysterious, but nonetheless acceptable. Job's words of faith in God resolved the problem for himself, even though he did not understand why: "Naked I came from my mother's womb, and naked shall I return; the Lord gave, and the Lord has taken away; blessed be the name of the Lord" (Job 1:21). Job's steadfastness in his faith and his patience with the Lord, even in times of great adversity, have often been pointed to by Christians as examples of the mystery of evil and the tapestry theory. Even the New Testament Letter of James refers to it with the following words: "You have heard of the steadfastness of Job, and you have seen the purpose of the Lord, how the Lord is compassionate and merciful" (Jas. 5:11). In this respect, many Christians have taken a more positive view of their suffering, realizing that it may be the avenue to new and creative heights for them. Others have not only looked upon it as a possible test from God himself, but as a means to personal improvement and maturity. Certainly suffering is an inevitable part of every person's life. What is important from the Christian point of view is the person's attitude toward suffering, not desiring it in itself, but rather attempting to turn its inevitability into a legitimate creative use.[44] Christian history is replete with examples of people who have made great contributions to humanity and the world out of their personal sufferings. In this sense too St. Paul wrote to the Romans the following: "We rejoice in our sufferings, knowing that suffering produces endurance, and endurance produces character, and character produces hope, and hope does not disappoint us, because God's love has been poured into our hearts through the Holy Spirit which has been given to us" (Rom. 5:3-5).

In general, Christians believe that the very structure of human history is basically a moral one. If people violate either the natural or moral laws governing their relationship and responsibility to the world, to themselves, and to others, they must pay the consequences. This violation can be done either personally or collectively and the sin that results wreaks havoc on human beings and their world. Human evil is thus the responsibility of human beings themselves and in their repentance they are required to try to undo the evil that they have generated by abusing their freedom. This rectification is not always easy to bring about, but nevertheless, people must make the effort if indeed their repentance is to be complete and sincere. In this respect, the contemporary world is still paying for the sins of its ancestors with regard to social and ecological evils prevalent in the world today. The example of a sincere Christian life can go a long way toward helping others live in accordance with the natural and moral laws. The problem remains, however, that neither the natural nor the moral laws are perfectly clear to people at all times because of the dynamic character of these laws. In general, however, they do support relationships of justice and love.

Notes - Chapter 6

1.Cf. the creation story in Gen. 1-2.

2.Cf. John B. Harrington, *Essentials in Christian Faith* (NY: Harper and Bros., 1958), 56-75.

3.Cf. Reinhold Niebuhr, *The Nature and Destiny of Man, I* (NY: Chas. Scribner's Sons, 1945), 12-18.

4.Cf. Macquarrie, *Principles of Christian Theology*, 62-63; Ignace Lepp, *The Authentic Morality* (NY: The Macmillan Co., 1965), 29-38; and Louis Monden, *Sin, Liberty and Law* (NY: Sheed and Ward, 1965), 19-30.

5.Cf. Lepp, *op. cit.*, 5-6.

6.Cf. Macquarrie, *Principles of Christian Theology*, 59-68.

7.Sin was expressed in traditional theological language by the Latin definition: *aversio a Deo et conversion ad creaturam*, a turning away from God toward a creature. P. Schoonenberg, *op. cit.*, p. 20 points out that this definition implies a "disordinate" turning toward a creature.

8.Cf., for example, Paul Ramsey, *Basic Christian Ethics* (NY: Chas Scribner's Sons, 1950), 290-344 and Charles E. Curran, *Christian Morality Today* (Notre Dame, IN: Fides Publishers, Inc., 1966), 5-6.

9.Cf. Bernhard Häring, *The Law of Christ, I* (Westminster, Md.: The Newman Press, 1961), 342-344 where Häring speaks of sin in terms of a biblical Greek word for it, *hamartia*, meaning loss of God.

10.Cf. *ibid.*, 344-346 where the biblical Greek word for sin, *anomia*, meaning opposition to the divine will expressed in the law, is explained.

11.Cf. *ibid.*, 346-348 where Häring explains the biblical Greek word for sin, *adikia*, in terms of a violation in justice owing to God.

12.For the social dimension of sin, cf. Ramsey's section on the "origin" of original sin, *op. cit.*, 306-325.

13.Cf., e.g., Ian G. Barbour, *Earth Might be Fair: Reflections on Ethics, Religion and Ecology* (Englewood Cliffs, NJ: Prentice-Hall, 1972) and John B. Cobb, Jr., *Is It Too Late? A Theology of Ecology* (Beverly Hills, CA:

Bruce, 1972).

14.Cf. Häring, *op. cit.*, 350-364.

15.Cf. *ibid.*, 348-350 and Niebuhr, *op. cit.*, 179-186.

16.Cf. Mt. 4:3.

17.Cf. Jas. 1:15.

18.Cf. Jn. 17:14; Rom. 5:12.

19.Cf. Lk. 22:40,46.

20.Cf. S. Dennis Ford, *Sins of Omission: A Primer on Moral Indifference* (Minneapolis, MN: Fortress Press, 1990) and Daniel C. Maguire, *The Moral Choice* (Garden City, NY: Doubleday and Co., Inc., 1978), 392-395.

21.As quoted in Ruth Zerner, "Martin Niemöller, Activist as Bystander: The Oft-Quoted Reflection," in *Jewish-Christian Encounters over the Centuries: Symbiosis, Prejudice, Holocaust, Dialogue*, ed. Marvin Perry and Frederick M. Schweitzer (NY: Peter Lang, 1994), 330.

22.Although this remark has been traditionally attributed to Edmund Burke, a bitter critic of the French Revolution, it is not found in any of his works. Perhaps it is a paraphrase of Burke's view published in 1770 that: "When bad men combine, the good must associate; else they will fall, one by one, an unpitied sacrifice in a contemptible struggle." Edmund Burke, *Thoughts on the Present Discontents and Speeches* (London,: Cassell & Co., Ltd., 1886), 114.

23.This definition of human beings viewing them as a result of certain positive and negative stimuli exerted upon them in a conditioning process is found in the more extreme forms of psychological behaviorism. Cf., e.g., B. F. Skinner, *Beyond Freedom and Dignity* (NY: Alfred A. Knopf, 1971).

24.Cf. Häring, *op. cit.*, 375.

25.For a study of these capital sins from the Roman Catholic perspective, cf. Häring, *op. cit.*, 374-382 and from the Protestant perspective, cf. Niebuhr, *op. cit.*, 186-240.

26.Mammon means material wealth or possessions.

27.Some of the evil results of excessive self-love are also delineated by St. Paul in the succeeding verses. Cf. Rom. 1:28-32.

28.Cf. Rom. 14:20-21 in this regard.

29.Cf. Eph. 4:26-27.

30.Cf. Jas. 1:19.

31.Sins of omission would largely follow from the vice of slothfulness.

32.Cf. Aquinas, *op. cit.*, I, 583-1161.

33.For example, the papal encyclical *Humanae Vitae*, issued by Pope Paul VI in 1968, banning artificial methods of contraception as a form of legitimate birth control for Roman Catholics reflected this type of teleological Thomistic approach. In this encyclical, Pope Paul VI insisted that "each and every marriage act must remain open to the transmission of life," the end or goal of sexual intercourse. Cf. Anthony Kosnik et al., *Human Sexuality: New Directions in American Catholic Thought* (NY: Paulist Press, 1977), 119-126.

34.The Ten Commandments are listed in two separate places in the Old Testament, Ex. 20:1-17 and Dt. 5:6-21.

35.Jesus' famous Sermon on the Mount is found in Mt. 5:1-7:29. Another version of it shows Jesus presenting this sermon on "a level place" in Lk. 6:17-49.

36.Cf. Maguire, *op. cit.*, 157-163.

37.Cf. Joseph Fletcher, *Situation Ethics* (Philadelphia: The Westminster Press, 1966), 18-22.

38.Cf. *ibid.*, 22-25.

39.Cf. *ibid.*, 26-37.

40.Cf. St. Augustine, *The City of God* ed. by Vernon J. Burke (NY: Doubleday and Co., 1958), 247-250. Cf. also St. Augustine, *Confessions* tr. by R. S. Pine-Coffin (Baltimore: Penguin Books, Inc., 1961), 59.

41.Cf. St. Athanasius, "On the Incarnation of the Word," *Library of the Christian Classics*, III, *Christology of the Later Fathers* ed. by Edward R. Hardy (Philadelphia: The Westminster Press, 1954), 59.

42.Cf. Gen. 1:31.

43.Cf. Augustine, *The City of God*, 247-250.

44.Cf. Gustave Thils, *Christian Holiness* (Tielt, Belgium: Lannoo Publishers, 1963), 577-579 and Austin Farrer, *Love Almighty and Ills Unlimited* (Garden City, NY: Doubleday and Co., Inc., 1961), 142-165.

Chapter 7

Christian Eschatology

As was pointed out earlier,[1] eschatology is the study of the last things and the last times, coming from the Greek word *eschatos* meaning last or extreme. Christian eschatology, therefore, deals principally with those Christian beliefs surrounding such concepts as death, judgment, heaven, and hell. It especially views these from the point of view of what Jesus has done for human beings. This Christological emphasis continually looks to Jesus in his role as prophet, priest, and king.[2] As prophet, Jesus speaks about God and his will for human beings which he certainly knows because he himself is the God-man. As priest, he has made it possible for people to be reunited with God and he incessantly seeks, as mediator, to reconcile sinners with God. As king, he has overcome evil and death, and Christians joined to him believe that they too can share in his victory over sin and death and live in his everlasting kingdom in heaven.

Christian faith embraces the ultimate destinies of the world and human beings based upon its belief in Jesus Christ, but much of its patent explicitness is not present because it deals with beliefs beyond the grave. For example, St. Paul wrote that: "No eye has seen, nor ear heard, nor the heart of man conceived, what God has prepared for those who love him" (I Cor. 2:9). Or as the author of St. John's First Letter wrote: "Beloved, we are God's children now; it does not yet appear what we shall be, but we know that when he appears we shall be like him, for we shall see him as he is" (I Jn. 3:2). Accordingly, as one would expect within the course of Christian history, much speculation is found surrounding these basic eschatological concepts. This wide spectrum of belief about the last times is reflected among the various Christian denominations.

A. The Concept of Death

Thanatology or the study of death has taken on a new importance in the contemporary world. Courses on death and dying are even found in the college curriculum today, indicating the interest that seems to surround this once taboo topic. Hospices for the care of those who are terminally ill are in existence around the world and the various stages of the dying process are studied by both professionals in the field of those caring for the dying as well as by non-professionals.[3] Some books have even been written about those persons who were clinically pronounced dead but were subsequently
resuscitated telling of their experience while they were in that apparent death state.[4] This fascination with death in the contemporary world is probably a healthy sign showing people's maturity in not being afraid to face the fact and certainty of death.

Yet the emphasis in contemporary western society still seems to embrace youth and life itself because of the vitality that is associated with it. Many funeral customs in western society also attempt to mask the reality of death. The establishment of retirement villages, old age homes, some nursing homes, and so on, show that society in general does not will to face too squarely the fact that indeed eventual death is a guaranteed reality that each person must face. The notion of putting old people out of society's view in general where they do not have everyday contact with young and middle-aged people is indeed a perverted view of life and death. Of course, at the other extreme was found the practice in some medieval monasteries of placing a skull and crossbones on the refectory table with the Latin words inscribed, *memento more,* "remember death."

The Christian approach to the subject of death is commonly found somewhere between these two extremes of a morbid preoccupation with the subject and the attempt to make it the forbidden topic of any reflection at all. The Christian's faith that Jesus has overcome death and that those who believe in Jesus will do likewise is a very reassuring doctrine of Christianity. However, this belief is in the realm of faith and any attempt to offer clinical evidence for the existence of an afterlife through scientific research dealing with the resuscitation of apparently dead people only serves to weaken the Christian faith position. This writer again must insist that well-meaning Christians should let faith be faith because the attempt to "prove" certain faith positions opens up Pandora's box to all kinds of justifiable criticisms of the Christian Faith. There are truly other plausible explanations to certain unexplained phenomena that can be and are given by those who operate with different sets of presuppositions.

1. *Death in the Old Testament.*[5] The Old Testament speaks of death fundamentally as the departure of the breath or divine spark from the earthly body. As Ninian Smart has written: "In the Old Testament, death is mainly regarded in a naturalistic way, as the dissolution of the individual."[6] This brings about the end of all earthly activity for the person, religious and otherwise, and involves the complete loss of vitality. Death is not viewed as being a particularly dreaded thing for those who have lived rather long lives, but only for the young. As a matter of fact, many Old Testament scholars interpret the lengthy ages given to particular persons in Old Testament history as signaling that the person was particularly good and God rewarded that person with a long life on earth.[7]

But death was not annihilation for the ancient Israelite. There is also the notion of survival after death present in the Old Testament literature in a realm called Sheol. It is in Sheol that the spirits of the dead reside in a rather strange, dreary, shadowy, meaningless existence. In Sheol all the departed dead are separated from the living and from God. No one comes back from Sheol.[8] However, one does not suffer in Sheol, nor does one receive certain rewards. It is a neutral and passive state.[9]

During late Old Testament times, the idea of resurrection gradually became a prominent belief among the Jews with the exception of the Sadducees. There was the notion that God will in some way conquer death, especially for those who remained faithful to him in life. Nevertheless, views on the afterlife remain nebulous as they do even for present day Judaism, which is much more concerned about this life and how it should be lived rather than speaking about death and the afterlife. Accordingly, there was no preoccupation with death and no developed theory of an afterlife among the ancient Israelites.[10]

2. *Death in the New Testament.*[11] In the New Testament, the predominant concern is not with death, but rather with life in Jesus Christ. There is the belief that death has been overcome by Jesus, as reflected in the New Testament Letter to Timothy that: "...our Savior, Christ, Jesus, abolished death and brought life and immortality to light through the gospel" (2 Tim. 1:10). Furthermore, Jesus is the first-born of the dead. He is seen as the "first fruits of those who have died" (1 Cor. 15:20). And if Jesus has not been raised from the dead, the faith of the Christian in general is ineffectual. In other words, all in Christianity revolves around the central and basic belief in the resurrection of Jesus. St. Paul made this clear while writing to the Corinthian church:

> Now if Christ is preached as raised from the dead, how can some of you
> say that there is no resurrection of the dead? But if there is no
> resurrection of the dead, then Christ has not been raised; if Christ has not
> been raised, then our preaching is in vain and your faith is in vain. (1 Cor.
> 15:12-14)

Because death is looked upon as a consequence of sin in the New
Testament,[12] and since Jesus has overcome sin and people's
estrangement with God through his atoning sacrifice, it follows that
death has been overcome as well. Therefore, for the Christian believer
following the teachings of the New Testament, death is not to be
feared, but to be embraced as leading to a new life with Jesus Christ.
At death, life is only changed, not taken away. With this religious
certitude, the Christian truly believes that: "Death is swallowed up in
victory" (1 Cor. 15:54).

   3. *Death in Christian Tradition.* Christian theologians have been
very much influenced in their understanding of death by Greek
philosophy.[13]
Whereas early Jewish-Christian thought sought to explain life after
death in terms of the resurrection of the body, Greek thought
understood life after death in terms of the immortality of the soul.
Traditional biblical thought about humans viewed them as a unity
consisting of an animated body, incarnate spirit, or psychophysical
entity. Greek philosophy tended to define humans as a duality of
body *and* soul. For example, the Greek philosopher, Plato, viewed the
pre-existent soul as residing in the prison of the body desiring to be
freed. Death brings about the freedom to be immortal and the purely
spiritual being that one wishes to be.[14] So, apparently influenced by
Greek philosophy, early Christian theologians added the notion of the
immortality of the soul after death, awaiting the future resurrection of
the body.

   Medieval Christian theologians also tended to be influenced by
Greek dualistic thought about death as well. Death was explained in
terms of a separation of the soul from the body. For example,
Aristotle, who exerted a great deal of influence upon the Scholastic
theologians, viewed the soul as the principle of life itself for the
body.[15] Christian theologians, attempting to reconcile the biblical and
Greek ways of thinking, taught that each individual soul was directly
created by God and after death goes to some intermediate state
awaiting the resurrection of its body at the final judgment and
permanent state of existence for all eternity. Roman Catholic, Eastern

Orthodox, and Protestant Christians only differed in their views regarding the intermediate state of the soul awaiting the general resurrection. However, the notion of a disembodied soul is no longer adhered to in much Christian theology today.

B. The Concept of Judgment

Just as the concepts of death and the life after death have undergone evolutionary change in the course of Christian tradition, so too has the notion of judgment after death.

1. *The New Testament Context of Judgment.* The New Testament speaks directly of only one judgment after death at the end of history. It is described as a general and summary judgment of all people by God after the resurrection of the dead at the *parousia*. This final or last judgment will decide the ultimate destiny of each person. According to the parable of the sheep and the goats in the New Testament, this judgment will find Jesus Christ returning in all of his glory to separate the saved from the damned.[16] The condemned "will go into eternal punishment, but the righteous into eternal life" (Mt. 25:46). This judgment will take place in the presence of all people.

2. *The Apostolic Fathers' Concept of Judgment.* Among the early Christian theologians there was retained the notion of the general, last, or final judgment. But since the *parousia* or the second coming of Christ had not transpired as yet, a question arose with regard to those who had already died. Where are they? Some of the early theologians reasoned, therefore, that there is a particular judgment made with respect to each individual soul immediately upon the death of one's body. For example, both Augustine[17] in the West and John Chrysostom[18] in the East emphasized two judgments for human beings, adding the notion of a particular judgment to the concept of the general judgment at Christ's return. However, many of the earlier Church Fathers[19] seem to have assumed a state of waiting between death and resurrection, in which the just are at rest and the evil are punished, but do not yet achieve the final happiness of Heaven or the final condemnation of Hell. Tertullian generally agreed, but he exempted martyrs whom he claimed immediately entered paradise upon death.[20]

3. *The Contemporary Concept of Judgment.* Belief in judgment after death, be it particular or general, is on the level of faith. There are both good and evil mixed together in the world, and the belief in

a judgment argues that good indeed will eventually win out and this will be proclaimed at the final judgment of all people. The parable of the wheat and the weeds in the New Testament illustrates this belief.[21] In the New Testament words of Jesus:

> The Son of man will send his angels, and they will gather out of his kingdom all causes of sin and all evildoers, and throw them into the furnace of fire; there men will weep and gnash their teeth. Then the righteous will shine like the sun in the kingdom of their Father. (Mt. 13:41-43)

Not all Christians, however, believe in the concept of two judgments after death. Whereas Roman Catholics, Eastern Orthodox Christians, and some Protestants embrace the belief in both a particular and a general judgment, other Protestant Christians only profess belief in a general judgment alone. To the question of what happens to those who die before the return of Jesus and the general judgment, the answer is given that these souls are asleep and resting in Abraham's bosom.[22] On the one hand, St. Paul suggests in his First Letter to the Church at Thessalonica[23] that there is something like a waiting sleep for all the dead until the general resurrection of the dead, and on the other hand, he writes to the church at Philippi[24] that he is torn between living and preaching the gospel or dying and being immediately with Christ. Furthermore, Jesus promised eternal life in his kingdom to the "good thief" on the cross who died the very day he did.[25] Therefore, the New Testament is indeed ambiguous on this question. However, those who profess belief in two judgments after death believe that all of the individual, particular judgments will be proclaimed publicly at the time of the general judgment and good will be decisively declared as the victor over evil.

C. Concept of Eternity

Life after death for the just has been described as eternal life. Basically, the concept of eternity implies that there is no beginning and there will be no end. For example, God is eternal insofar as God always existed and always will exist. For God to die or go out of existence would be against his own perfection as God. However, human beings are described as being immortal. They are created beings who come into existence by God's will, but they will never lose their existence even at death. They will go on existing in the afterlife for all eternity. Mortal beings are those lower beings who are created but who also pass out of existence at death.

They have both a beginning in time and an end in time without any immortality. With this understanding of eternity and eternal life, Christians tend to speak of death in terms of passing on into that life after the grave, which is characterized by endless duration. Life begun here on this earth continues after death into eternity.

While comparing life before and after the grave, Christians also distinguish between temporality and eternity. Whereas life on this earth is lived in the succession of time, life after death is continued without the succession of time in a state of timelessness. Inasmuch as life on this earth is lived amid change where there is growth and decay, life after death involves no change as such as is found in temporal, mutable existence. In eternity, therefore, there is no before or after, only timeless existence, an endless now or present.

It should also be mentioned that for some Christians the notion of eternity implies participating in God's own life after death. Not having achieved this at death puts a person in the realm of nothingness and non-existence. Therefore, this position concludes that immortality is actually based upon the acceptance of the gift of salvation or not.[26] If this gift or grace is not accepted, then the person at death passes into a state where his or her being is negated. In other words, that person literally goes out of existence. To the question of whether or not human beings are immortal, the answer is given that immortality is indeed possible but not certain. Its possibility is based upon a person's fulfillment of his or her being given to him or her as designed by God. Non-fulfillment results in the annihilation of that person's potential for existence, and that person remains a mere mortal without immortality. Eternal life and immortality are not something that human beings have a right to, rather they are gifts freely given by God. And as with any gift, they may be accepted or rejected.

D. Concepts of Heaven, Hell, and Purgatory

In the New Testament Jesus clearly speaks of what will happen to those people who accept or reject God's will for them.[27] Traditionally, life after death has been spoken of using the images of Heaven, Hell, and Purgatory. These concepts are among the most difficult of the eschatological ideas to discuss because they have become entangled in so much mythological imagery throughout the years.

1. *Concept of Heaven.* Heaven may be defined as the goal of human existence. It involves an eternal life of living the fulness of one's

humanity freely and genuinely. It is the life originally willed for human beings by their creator. Heaven then is the life that is achieved after death by one who lived a life of faith, hope, and love on this earth. The relationship the person in Heaven will have with God will be essentially the same that the person had with God on earth, but it will be a much more intense and complete relationship. The continuity between Heaven and earth is found expressed in the words of Jesus: "Truly, truly, I say to you, he who hears my word and believes him who sent me, has eternal life; he does not come into judgment, but has passed from death to life" (Jn. 5:24). This life after death is life with and in God.

Heaven has also been described as Paradise, reflecting the perfect state that God established for humans at the beginning of creation. As a matter of fact, Jesus employed this term when promising salvation to the "good thief" on the cross at the time of his crucifixion: "Truly, I say to you, today you will be with me in Paradise" (Lk. 23:43). Another expression that has been used especially by Roman Catholic theologians to describe Heaven is the idiom, Beatific Vision. This term attempts to describe the reality of Heaven by indicating that the saved person has an immediate and clear vision of God. As St. Paul wrote to the Corinthian Church: "For now we see in a mirror dimly, but then face to face" (I Cor. 13:12). Still others prefer to speak of Heaven as a state of rest. This does not mean to imply that in Heaven people lounge around doing nothing forever, but it means being at rest from the frustrations, tensions, conflicts, and so on found in life on this side of the grave. It means being at rest with oneself as well as with others in a state of abiding love, peace, joy, and happiness.[28] The remainder is mystery. The absolute maturity of people in Heaven is matched by the superabundance of good things heaped upon the saved in Heaven. As St. Paul attempted to describe Heaven: "No eye has seen, nor ear heard, nor the heart of man conceived, what God has prepared for those who love him" (1 Cor. 2:9).

2. *Concept of Hell.* The quality of life in Hell differs a great deal from the quality of life found in Heaven. If Heaven is the goal of human existence involving the living for eternity the fullness of one's humanity, Hell may be understood as an eternal life of living one's unfulfilled humanity, having lost the fundamental goal of human existence. This involves the state of living forever in estrangement and hostility toward God and one's fellow human beings. This includes not being at rest with oneself or with anyone else in a state of alienation, hate, frustration, tension, conflict, and so on. Hell is simply the working out of unrepentant sin for all eternity.

In traditional Christian theology, Hell has been described as a permanent state of damnation for unrepentant sinners after death. This understanding of Hell as a possible permanent state after death certainly receives support from the words of Jesus in the New Testament:

> And if your hand causes you to sin, cut it off; it is better for you to enter life maimed than with two hands to go to Hell, to the unquenchable fire. And if your foot causes you to sin, cut it off; it is better for you to enter life lame than with two feet to be thrown into Hell. And if your eye causes you to sin, pluck it out; it is better for you to enter the kingdom of God with one eye than with two eyes to be thrown into Hell, where their worm does not die, and the fire is not quenched. (Mk. 9:43-48)

This "unquenchable fire" of Hell certainly does conjure up the notion that Hell is definitely permanent.

However, some Christians from early times have argued that Hell may be either permanent or impermanent. They maintain that the repentant sinner in Hell never gets beyond the reconciling efforts of God, that God's reconciling activity cannot and should not be restricted to only a person's life on earth. Therefore, the notion of a Hell where the wicked are forever punished by God without any hope for reconciliation of the sinner with God seems incongruous with God's perfection.[29] God wills that all human beings achieve the merits of the atonement of Jesus Christ and will never give up his efforts to bring about universal reconciliation. Of course, this also demands the free cooperation of the sinner as well. In the New Testament Letter to Timothy, it states that: "This is good, and it is acceptable in the sight of God our Savior, who desires all men to be saved and to come to the knowledge of the truth" (1 Tim. 2:3-4). Therefore, certain theologians leave open the question regarding the finality and irrevocability of Hell and espouse the notion of another chance to achieve salvation even after the grave.

As with the idea of Heaven, so too do Christians affirm that there is continuity between life on earth and torment in Hell. The lack of love, the alienation a person experiences on earth, and the inauthenticity of one's existence on earth all carry over into the afterlife of the damned. The non-acceptance of God's saving grace does indeed make a person's life on earth miserable and this misery is compounded in the torment of Hell, everlasting or not. Traditionally this punishment in Hell has been described especially in terms of "fire and brimstone." This description is taken from the Book of Revelation[30] in the New Testament, as well as from the words of Jesus such as those already cited above from St. Mark's

Gospel.[31] The real punishment of Hell, however, is one of loss and unfulfillment. The person in Hell did not achieve the goal of human existence itself and it would have been better had that person not been born.[32]

3.*Concept of Purgatory*. Purgatory, a doctrine of Roman Catholicism, refers to an intermediate state between Heaven and Hell. It is the process by which a person, after death, becomes eligible for Heaven. Therefore, according to Roman Catholic belief, unrepented venial sins and the temporal punishment due to forgiven sins must be made up for in Purgatory before that person can enter Heaven.[33] People dying in the unrepentant state of mortal sin are consigned to everlasting Hell.[34] The person in Purgatory is ultimately assured of Heaven, but cannot enter Heaven directly because of the imperfect nature of that person's relationship with God at the time of death.

The majority of Protestant Christians generally reject the doctrine of Purgatory primarily because they maintain that it is not taught in the Bible. Roman Catholics, however, claim that it is taught in their Old Testament Second Book of Maccabees, which affirms that it is a good deed to pray for the dead so that their sins might be forgiven.[35] In other words, to pray for the dead means that they can be helped out of their suffering and impermanent state after death. Roman Catholics also emphasize that Christian tradition from very early times taught the notion of an intermediate state between Heaven and Hell.[36] Those Christians who reject the belief in Purgatory also object that it suggests that the satisfaction of Jesus Christ's atonement is not fully sufficient for the remission of sins and that there is retained the concept of punishment even after one's sins are forgiven. This criticism is especially directed to the Roman Catholic belief in temporal punishment that the sinner must make up for, even after a sin has been forgiven and the eternal punishment taken away. Through prayer, good works, or by the reception of an indulgence[37] from the church this temporal punishment due to one's sins can be alleviated. If not, suffering in Purgatory is mandatory.

Truly the belief in Purgatory is associated with suffering. This suffering, which will eventually come to an end and can be lessened by the prayers and good works of those still living on earth, consists of the person being more conformed to Jesus Christ in perfect love and obedience to God's will.[38] This process is one of purging and purification. In this respect, the belief in Purgatory is analogous to the belief mentioned above concerning the impermanence of Hell.

Just as Heaven and Hell are experienced in varying degrees in one's life on this earth, so too does Purgatory belong to one's experience this side of the grave. Again there is continuity found between the two. By suffering the effects in time of one's sins on earth, one is already involved in the process of making up for one's temporal punishment. This involves the continual dying to oneself and to one's own selfish desires and the rising to live the new life in Christ Jesus which is eternal life itself. This struggle is found in the daily lives of people who are indeed sinners.[39]

E. The End of History

According to traditional Christian belief, the original source and beginning of all in history was God, the creator. God created all creatures that exist, including those with human existence. God's revelation through his Chosen People, the Jews, prepared humans for the incarnation of the Son of God as the Messiah. Jesus Christ atoned for all the sins of humanity. From that time forward, human beings have had the choice of either accepting or rejecting that gift of salvation. At the same time, people in every generation are looking forward to the very end of history and time itself when the kingdom of God will be definitively established and the ultimate triumph of good, love, and justice will be made known to all. This end of history is the primary object of the Christian's hope in every age and is associated with the second coming of Jesus Christ in his glory to judge all people. The technical term employed to describe this phenomenon of faith is the Greek word, *parousia*, meaning "coming" or "presence" as it is used in the New Testament.[40] The goal of history from the Christian point of view is found in the *parousia*, no matter how it is interpreted.

Apparently, many of the earliest Christians believed that the end of history would occur in their own lifetimes or soon thereafter. For example, St. Paul in his earlier writings expected the end to occur very soon.[41] But in his later writings, he seemed to postpone the end of history to an indefinite future.[42] Jesus' words on this issue are also rather ambiguous. On the one hand, he seems to have thought that the end of history and the resurrection of the dead would come quite soon,[43] and on the other hand, he explicitly taught that: "Of that day or that hour no one knows, not even the angels in Heaven, nor the Son, but only the Father" (Mk. 13:32). Both the Apostles' and the Nicene Creeds explicitly profess belief in a Christ who will return and judge the living and the dead.

In more contemporary times, much of liberal Protestantism has rejected the notion of a literal second coming of Jesus.[44] They tend to view the *parousia* as a symbol which teaches that history has an end and a goal which involves a judgment on sin. Evil does not ultimately win out, but will be definitively put down by goodness found in the redemptive power of Jesus Christ. However, for those who do believe in a literal second coming of Jesus, there are different points of view. Associated with the attempts to foretell his actual return are Christian movements generally referred to by the term millennialism which is derived from the Latin word for a thousand. Millennialist views are largely based upon interpretations of the thousand year reign of Christ referred to in the New Testament Book of Revelation.[45] Millennialism is sometimes also called chiliasm from the Greek word meaning a thousand.

Those Christians who are most inclined to take biblical prophecies concerning the return of Christ literally are the premillennialists.[46] Generally, they believe that before the second coming of Christ occurs there will be much evil and tribulation found in the world, including the appearance of the Antichrist. This will be followed by a millennium of Christ's reign upon earth characterized by peace and order. At the end of this millennium the Devil and the forces of evil will once again be set loose in the world. Then there will be a final judgment at which the Devil and all of his wicked, evil followers will be committed to the everlasting punishment of Hell. Some premillennialists believe that a phenomenon called the secret rapture or translation will occur before, during, or after the series of calamities and tribulations of the last days.[47] This rapture involves the snatching of God's saints out of the mass of humanity to rule with Jesus Christ. Those who especially believe in the rapture are more fundamentalist type Protestant Christians who refer to themselves as dispensationalists. They take this name from their belief that God's dealings with the world are divided into different periods or dispensations of history.[48] Usually seven dispensations or periods of time are isolated: 1) Innocence (Adam and Eve); 2) Conscience (Adam-Noah); 3) Government (Noah-Abraham); 4) Calling and Promise (Abraham-Moses); 5) Legislation (Moses-Jesus); 6) Grace (Jesus-Jesus' Return); and 7) Kingdom (Millennial Kingdom).

Those Christians who believe that the millennium will precede the *parousia* of Christ are called postmillennialists.[49] They interpret the biblical prophecies to teach that there will be a golden age of the Church of Christ under which humans will experience unusual peace and prosperity. This millennium of peace and prosperity will be followed by a conflict between good and evil and the return of Jesus Christ. This interpretation was most fashionable during the prevailing optimism of the nineteenth century.

A third position found among Christians who believe in a literal second coming of Christ teaches that the one-thousand years of the millennium are symbolic.[50] Some think that they are symbolic of Christ's eternal, heavenly reign. Others assert that they symbolize the period between the first and second comings of Christ in which the Kingdom of God already exists but is only partially realized. These non-millennialists or a-millennialists believe the *parousia* or the second coming of Christ can occur at any time at all and they equate the interim of life on earth with the tribulations of the last days.

It would seem that movements of millennialism correspond to times of misfortune, tribulation, and pessimistic periods of human history.[51] In this respect, interest in millennialism is similar to the rise of the apocalyptic literature both within the Bible and outside of it. The word apocalyptic is derived from the Greek word meaning to unfold or reveal and apocalyptic literature is usually written in times of rather extreme suffering and persecution.[52] It is meant to help the faithful ones endure even throughout their suffering because better and more promising times lie ahead, especially for those who persevere in their faith. It might also be mentioned that beliefs in Satanism and atheism seem to abound in periods of history characterized by extreme pessimism. Things are looked upon as being so bleak that belief in God is either replaced by belief in Satan as the dominant power in the world or no belief in a Supreme Being at all.

Be that as it may, Christians even in the bleakest of periods have clung to their hope with regard to their belief that Jesus has overcome evil and that the end of history will definitely make this belief apparent to all people. They look forward to the fulfillment of the created world in terms of a "new heaven and a new earth" (Rev. 21:1). They also look forward to the completion and perfection of their own humanity.[53] This is the good news that Christians wish to share with others about the future. The end of history for them is eagerly awaited, not in terms of finality but rather in terms of the expectation of fulfillment. Truly the end of history is the goal and purpose of creation itself. Christians daily pray for the realization of the Kingdom of God using the words of the Lord's Prayer,[54] "Thy Kingdom come." Some also frequently exclaim the Aramaic expression *Maranatha*"[55] (Our Lord, come!).

Notes - Chapter 7

1.Cf. *supra*, pp. 73-75.

2.Christian thought traditionally has described Jesus' person and work as that of prophet, priest, and king.

3.Cf., e.g., Elizabeth Kübler-Ross, *On Death and Dying* (NY: The Macmillan Co., 1969). For a good overview of current practices dealing with death and dying, cf. David Dempsey, *The Way We Die: An Investigation of Death and Dying in America Today (NY: Macmillan Publishing Co., Inc., 1975).*

4.Cf., e.g., Raymond A. Moody, *Life After Life* (NY: Bantam Books, Inc., 1977), Maurice Rawlings, *Beyond Death's Door* (NY: Bantam Books, Inc., 1981), and Lee W. Bailey and Jenny Yates (eds.), *The Near-Death Experience: A Reader* (NY: Routledge, 1996).

5.Cf. Lou H. Silberman, "Death in the Hebrew Bible and Apocalyptic Literature," *Perspectives on Death*, ed. by Liston O. Mills (Nashville: Abingdon Press, 1969), 13-32. Cf. also Paul Heinisch, *Theology of the Old Testament*, tr. by Wm. G. Heidt (St. Paul: The North Central Publishing Co., 1955), 279-294 and Ninian Smart, "Death in the Judaeo-Christian Tradition," in Arnold Toynbee et al., *Man's Concern with Death* (St. Louis: McGraw-Hill Book Co., 1969), 116-121.

6.N. Smart, *op. cit.*, 116.

7.Cf. Robert H. Pfeiffer, *Introduction to the Old Testament* (London: Adam and Charles Black, Ltd., 1953), 199-200.

8.Cf. 2 Sam. 12:23.

9.Cf., e.g., Job 10:21-22; Ps. 6:5; 88:4-6, 10-12, and Is. 38:18-19.

10.Cf. M. S. Miller and J. L. Miller, *op. cit.*, 131.

11.Cf. Leander E. Keck, "New Testament Views of Death," *Perspectives on Death*, ed. by L. O. Mills, (Nashville: Abingdon Press, 1969), 33-98. Cf. also Rudolf Bultmann, *Theology of the New Testament*, I, 345-352.

12.Cf. Rom. 5:12.

13.Cf. Krister Stendahl, ed., *Immortality and Resurrection* (NY: The Macmillan Co., 1965)and N. Smart, *op. cit.*, 118-119.

14.This is why the Greeks in the Areopagus at Athens were very interested in what St. Paul was preaching to them about the Gospel of Jesus Christ until: "When they heard of the resurrection of the dead, some scoffed; but others said, 'We will hear you again about this'"(Acts 17:32). The resurrection of the dead was unreasonable to them because by their belief at death one's soul was liberated from the prison of the body. Why would one wish for one's soul to return to this prison with the resurrection of one's body? Cf. Acts: 17:22-34 for the complete biblical pericope.

15.Cf. Jacques Maritain, *The Range of Reason* (NY: Charles Scribner's Sons, 1952), 54-61.

16.Cf. Mt. 25:31-46.

17.Cf. St. Augustine, "On the Soul and Its Origin," *A Select Library of the Nicene and Post-Nicene Fathers of the Christian Church*, ed. by Philip Schaff, V (Grand Rapids, MI: Wm. B. Eerdmans Pub. Co., 1956), 334.

18.Cf. St. John Chrysostom, "Homily XIV, Matt. 4:12," *Ibid.*, X, 90.

19.These would include Church Fathers such as St. Justin, St. Irenaeus, St. Ambrose, etc.

20.Cf. Tertullian, "On the Resurrection of the Flesh," *The Ante-Nicene Fathers*, ed. by A. Roberts and J. Donaldson, III (Grand Rapids, MI: Wm. B. Eerdmans Pub. Co., 1956), 576.

21.Cf. Mt. 13:24-30, 36-43.

22.Cf. Lk. 16:22 and 1 Th. 4:13-18.

23.Cf. 1 Th. 4:13-18.

24.Cf. Phil. 1:23.

25.Cf. Lk. 23:43.

26.This belief is usually known as conditional immortality.

27.Cf. Mt. 25:31-46.

28.Cf. Heb. 4:1-13 and 2 Th. 1:6-7.

29.Traditionally, this view, which claims that all creation will ultimately be saved, was called *apocatastasis*, a Greek word meaning "restoration." It was defended by such early theologians as Origen and others. Cf. Karl Rahner, *Theological Dictionary* (NY: Herder and Herder, 1965), 30-31; J. Macquarrie, *Principles of Christian Theology*, 326-327; and N. Smart, *op. cit.*, 120. Smart writes: "Origen's works had become available again in the 16th century. A number of the more radical Protestant movements, such as the Anabaptists and the Moravians, considerably modified the traditional teaching about hell. The former, for instance, treated hell as purgatory: thus eventually all would attain salvation (though admittedly there was much suffering to go through for most folk). The Socinians argued for the annihilation of the wicked, as indeed do some modern sects: that is, the wicked would simply die at death---only the saved would be raised to joy." (p. 120)

30.Cf. Rev. 20:10.

31.Cf. Mk. 9:43-48.

32.Cf. Mt. 26:24.

33. "All who die in God's grace and friendship, but still imperfectly purified, are indeed assured of their eternal salvation; but after death they undergo purification, so as to achieve the holiness necessary to enter the joy of Heaven." *Catechism of the Catholic Church*, 268, §1030. Cf. also Ott, *op. cit.*, 482-485.

34. "To die in mortal sin without repenting and accepting God's merciful love means remaining separated from him for ever by our own free choice. This state of definitive self-exclusion from communion with God and the blessed is called 'Hell.'" *Catechism of the Catholic Church*, 269, §1033.

35.Cf. 2 Macc. 12:42-46. The Books of Maccabees found in Roman Catholic and Eastern Orthodox bibles are regarded as being apocryphal or noncanonical writings by Protestant Christians. Eastern Orthodoxy also teaches that some kind of intermediate state exists after death in which a person can be helped by the prayers and sacrifices of those people still alive on earth.

36.Cf. Ott, *op. cit.*, 484 and *Catechism of the Catholic Church*, 268-269, §1031, §1032.

37 "An indulgence is a remission before God of the temporal punishment due to sins whose guilt has already been forgiven, which the faithful Christian who is duly disposed gains under certain prescribed conditions through the action of the Church which, as the minister of redemption, dispenses and applies with authority the treasury of the satisfactions of Christ and the saints." Pope Paul VI, apostolic constitution, *Indulgentiarum doctrina*, Norm 1 as quoted in *Catechism of the Catholic Church*, 370, §1471. "'An indulgence is partial or plenary according as it removes either part or all of the temporal punishment due to sin.' Indulgences may be applied to the living or the dead." *Ibid*.

38.Cf. Romano Guardini, *The Last Things* (London: Burns and Oates, 1954), 44-49.

39.Cf. Thils, *op. cit.*, 573-581.

40.Cf., e.g., 2 Th. 2:1.

41.Cf. 1 Th. 4:13-18.

42.Cf. Rom. 9-11.

43.Cf. Mk. 13:30.

44.Cf. Paul Tillich, *Systematic Theology*, II (NY: Harper and Row, 1967), 163-164.

45.Cf. Rev. 20:2-8.

46.Cf., e.g., George Eldon Ladd, *The Last Things* (Grand Rapids, MI: Wm. B. Eerdmans Publishing Co., 1978) for a rather thorough explanation of the premillennialist position.

47.Cf. *Ibid., 84-85*.

48.Cf. Hal Lindsey, *The Late Great Planet Earth* (Grand Rapids, MI: Zondervan Publishing House, 1970), 43 where Lindsey predicted while interpreting Mt. 24:34 that the rapture would likely come within the "generation" (40 years) of those who were alive for the 1948 founding of Israel. Edgar C. Whisenant also was of a similar expectation when he published his *88 Reasons Why the Rapture Could be in 1988* (Nashville: World Bible Society, 1988). However, G. E. Ladd, *op. cit.*, 19-28 denied that this could be ascertained from the study of the New Testament.

49.Cf. Ernest R. Sandeen, *The Roots of Fundamentalism: British and American Millenarianism 1800-1930* (Chicago: University of Chicago Press, 1970), 5, 43, 46.

50.Cf. Alois Winklhofer, *The Coming of His Kingdom: A Theology of the Last Things* (Edinburgh-London: Nelson, 1963), 159-160; 173-176.

51.Cf. Michael Barkun *Disaster and the Millennium* (New Haven: Yale University Press, 1974) and M. S. and J. L. Miller, *op. cit.*, 445.

52.Cf. M. S. and J. L. Miller, *op. cit.*, 23-24.

53.Cf. 2 Cor. 5:17; Eph. 2:15.

54.The Lord's Prayer, also known as the "Our Father" or "*Pater Noster*" is the prayer Jesus gave to his disciples when he said: "Pray then like this: Our Father who art in heaven, hallowed be thy name. Thy kingdom come, Thy will be done, on earth as it is in heaven. Give us this day our daily bread; and forgive us our debts, as we also have forgiven our debtors; and lead us not into temptation, but deliver us from evil." (Mt. 6:9-13).

55.*Maranatha* is an Aramaic prayer apparently used by the primitive Christian community to express its longing for Jesus' return. It is generally translated as: "Our Lord, come!" Cf. 1 Cor. 16:22 where St. Paul employs this petition.

Glossary

Agnosticism: The faith position taken by those persons who claim they do not have enough knowledge to be certain about the existence of God.

Angel: The word "angel" is derived from a Greek word meaning messenger. Angels are seen as heavenly beings who are intermediaries between God and humans.

Animism: The belief that all nature is alive and filled with unseen souls or spirits which may be worshiped or placated.

Annunciation: The event described in the Gospel of Luke 1:26-38 portraying the angel, Gabriel, as appearing to Mary in Nazareth and announcing to her that she was to become the mother of Jesus.

Anthropomorphism: The attribution of human characteristics, activities, or emotions to God.

Anti Christ: The word used by the author of the Johannine Epistles for those who deny Christ (1 Jn. 2:18-22; 2 Jn. 7). The term is often used with reference to the demonic forces of evil that will appear before the second coming of Christ based upon various readings of the Book of Revelation.

Antinomianism: The view that claims that people are not bound by any laws and so are free from all moral obligations or principles.

Apocalypticism: Derived from a Greek word meaning "revelation" or "unveiling," it is a religious movement that claims to reveal things which are normally hidden and lie in the future.

Apocatastasis: A Greek word referring to the final and complete salvation of all beings and is equated with universal salvation.

Apologetics: A reasoned defense of one's faith position.

Apostasy: An abandonment of one's religious faith.

Apostle: Refers to the original twelve disciples of Jesus whom he sent out to preach the gospel to others. The Greek word *apostolos* means "messenger."

Apostles' Creed: A summary of the faith and beliefs of Jesus' original apostles which became the ancient baptismal creed or symbol of the Church at Rome.

Arianism: A heresy named after a priest of Alexandria, Arius (c.250-c.336), and condemned by the Council of Nicaea in 325. This christological heresy advocated that Jesus was not truly divine.

Ascension: The belief that Jesus Christ proceeded to heaven after his resurrection from the dead.

Asceticism: The practice of austere self-discipline from religious motives.

Atheism: The positive belief in the non-existence of God.

Atonement: The restoration of the broken relationship between God and humans that was accomplished by the life and death of Jesus Christ.

Attributes of God: Those characteristics uniquely applicable to God.

Authentic Existence: A term used by existentialists to denote genuine human existence coming about because of deliberate choices or decisions made by human beings to be who they are and can be.

Baptism: A word derived from the Greek word *baptizein* which means to "immerse." It is the initiatory ritual or sacrament of the Christian church.

Beatific Vision: The goal of the Christian religion when a person after death has the immediate vision of God in heaven.

Being: Existence or one that exists.

Bible: The sacred scriptures/writings of Christianity including the books of both the Old Testament and the New Testament.

Bishop: The title (Gk. *episcopos/overseer*) applied to the highest order one can receive in some Christian clergy. Bishops are viewed as the ordained successors of Jesus' original Apostles and are distinguished from priests chiefly by their power to confer ordination or holy Orders.

Blasphemy: Any speech, act, or thought which dishonors or defames the nature or name of God.

Body of Christ: Another name for the church or the consecrated bread and wine one receives in Holy Communion.

Calvary: From the Latin word "*calvaria*" which means skull and refers to Golgotha (from an Aramaic word meaning "skull") near Jerusalem where Jesus was crucified.

Casuistry: The application of general moral principles to concrete cases or matters of ethical decision.

Catechism: An instructional summary of the basic beliefs and teachings of a religion usually in question-and-answer form.

Catholic: A word derived from a Greek word meaning universal.

Charism: A word derived from the Greek word *kharisma* meaning divine gift or favor.

Charity: A word that is sometimes used to translate the Greek word *agapé* which means love. Along with faith and hope, charity/love is regarded as one of the three theological virtues.

Chiliasm: A word that comes from a Greek word meaning a thousand and is a synonym for millennialism.

Christ: The transliteration of the Greek word *christos* which means messiah.

Christology: That part of Christian theology that is concerned with the study of Jesus Christ.

Christmas: The Christian festival that annually celebrates the birthday of Jesus on December 25th.

Church: The universal community of believers who have undergone Christian conversion having been called together by God.

Clergy: People who are set aside and ordained for religious service in the church.

Concupiscence: The inordinate desire for worldly and fleshly goals which has its location in the human senses.

Conscience: The human faculty that judges one's own actions to be right or wrong.

Contrition: Sincere sorrow for having sinned against God with the resolution never to sin again.

Conversion: The conscious act of accepting a religious faith.

Covenant: A pact, treaty, agreement, or testament between two parties.

Creation: The act of bringing something into existence where previously nothing existed.

Creed: A word derived from the Latin word *credo* meaning "I believe." It refers to a statement of the essential articles of a religious belief.

Crucifixion: A Roman means of capital punishment at the time of Christ whereby a person was suspended from a cross until the victim died. The cross consisted of an upright post with a transverse beam near the top.

Deacon: A title translated from the Greek *diakonos* which means servant or minister. It refers to a rank in some Christian clergy which is below both a bishop and a priest. Deacons are ordained to serve the Christian community as seven men were chosen to assist the Apostles in Acts 6:1-6.

Decalogue: The name given to the Ten Commandments traditionally believed to have been given to Moses on Mt. Sinai.

Deism: The belief that God is the intelligent creator of the world but does not providentially guide or intervene in any way with its course or destiny.

Demythologization: A type of biblical interpretation that views the Bible as composed of religious myths or stories that need to be interpreted for the religious truths they contain.

Deontological: Refers to an ethic constructed only on moral obligation and duty in contrast to an ethic based upon consequences or ends.

Determinism: The mechanical view that all events, including human action, are determined by causes regarded as external to the human will.

Demon: A devil or evil spirit.

Devil: A word from the Greek *diabolos* meaning accuser or slanderer. Also called Satan and is the major evil spirit in Christian theology.

Dispensationalism: A school of Christian belief that divides the history of creation into different periods of times or "dispensations" characterized by categories of God's major interventions.

Docetism: A Christological theory that advocates that Jesus' humanity only appeared or seemed human but was not really human.

Dogma: A system of official beliefs proclaimed by a church as normative for its members.

Dualism: All existence is viewed in term of two distinct realities.

Easter Sunday: The annual celebration of Jesus' resurrection from the dead.

Ecumenism: The modern Christian movement that searches and works for Christian unity.

Ekklesia: The Greek word used in the New Testament to designate the church.

Elohim: A plural form of *"el"* used in the Old Testament and one of the names by which the God of the biblical patriarchs was known.

Epiphany: The festival that annually celebrates the visit of the Magi/Wise Men from the East to the baby Jesus after his birth in Bethlehem.

Eschatology: The study of the last things/times.

Essence: That which makes anything that which it is; the nature of anything.

Essenes: A Jewish sect at the time of Jesus who lived in communes and practiced rigorous asceticism preparing themselves for the coming of the Messiah.

Eternity: Existence without beginning or end.

Ethics: The study of what is morally right and wrong.

Eucharist: A word derived from a Greek word meaning "thanksgiving" and refers to the Christian sacrament commemorating Christ's Last Supper. It is also called the Lord's Supper or Holy Communion.

Existence: The actuality rather than the potentiality in time and space of any subject.

Existentialism: A philosophical theory emphasizing the existence of the individual person as freely and responsibly choosing his/her own essence.

Exorcism: The ritual of expelling Satan/the Devil or a demon from a person, place or thing.

Faith: Belief in God.

Fundamentalism: A religious movement that bases its position on the literal interpretation of the books of the Bible and emphasizes the defining and defending of its essential beliefs.

Glossolalia: The ecstatic state of speaking in tongues inspired by a gift or charism of the Holy Spirit.

Gnosticism: An early Christian heresy that professed belief in a secret knowledge (Gk. *gnosis*) leading to salvation.

God: The proper name for the deity or Ultimate Reality in Christianity.

Golgotha: From the Aramaic word for "skull" and refers to the hill near Jerusalem where Jesus was crucified. Calvary.

Gospel: The good news of salvation preached by Jesus Christ.

Grace: The free and unmerited gift that God gives to humans restoring their good relationship with him. A state of friendship rather than estrangement with God.

Heaven: The abode of God, the angels, and the saints. Paradise.

Hell: The state of utter and irrevocable damnation to which a person not in a state of friendship with God is condemned after death.

Henotheism: The belief in many gods one of whom is superior to all the others.

Heresy: A doctrine or belief at variance with established beliefs or doctrines of the church.

Holy: Set apart from evil and identified with God.

Holy Communion: *See* Eucharist.

Holy Ghost: Archaic name for the Holy Spirit referring to the third person in God.

Holy Spirit: The third person of the triune God. Also called Holy Ghost.

Hypostasis: A Greek term for "person" used with reference to the persons of the Trinity.

Hypostatic Union: The technical term for the union of the divine and human natures in the one person of Jesus Christ.

Immortality: The belief that although human existence had a beginning, it will have no end and will continue even after death.

Incarnation: The belief that the Son of God became flesh in Jesus Christ.

Indulgence: The Roman Catholic practice of the remission of temporal punishment due for a sin after the eternal punishment and guilt have been forgiven.

Inquisition: A former Roman Catholic tribunal directed at the suppression of heresy.

Inspiration: Refers to the influence of the Holy Spirit upon humans.

Israelites: The descendants of Abraham, Isaac, and Jacob in biblical times.

Jesus Christ: The Son of God and the second person in the triune God who became flesh and is recognized as the promised Messiah.

Juridical: Of or pertaining to the law.

Justification: Refers to that act by which God brings a person back into proper relationship with himself. Undergoing conversion or the achieving of righteousness.

***Kairos*:** A Greek word used in the New Testament for time to distinguish chronological time (*chronos*) from the time a person has in his/her life to make ultimately significant decisions.

***Kenosis*:** A word derived from the Greek word meaning "to empty" and refers to the theory that when the Son of God became human he emptied himself of his divinity and did not reassume it until his resurrection from the dead.

***Kerygma*:** A word derived from the Greek verb meaning "to proclaim" and used in Christian theology to refer to the proclaimed message found in the essence of the Gospel of Jesus Christ.

Kingdom of God: A term used in Christian theology to refer to God's reign and rule over his creation.

***Koinonia*:** A word used in the New Testament to refer to the community of Christians joined together in Christ.

Laity: A word that is used to distinguish members in the church from the clergy.

Legalism: The ethical position that advocates strict, literal adherence to the law.

***Logos*:** The Greek term for "word" used in the Gospel of John with reference to the Son of God's existence before he became human.

Lord's Supper: *See* Eucharist.

Magi: Those men from the East who visited Jesus after his birth in Bethlehem. They presented Jesus with gifts of gold, frankincense, and myrrh. Also called the Wise Men. *See* Epiphany.

Mariology: The study of Mary in her role as the mother of Jesus.

Martyr: Derived from the Greek word for "witness," the word refers to a person who suffers death because of his or her beliefs.

Messiah: From a word in Hebrew *mashiah* meaning "anointed one." At the time of Jesus, the Jews anticipated a king who would be anointed by God and deliver them from their Roman oppression. Jesus was recognized by his followers as fulfilling Old Testament messianic prophecies and occupying this role. The Greek word for Messiah is *Khristos* and is transliterated by Christians into "Christ."

Messianism: The movement in Judaism throughout the ages dealing with messianic expectation.

***Metanoia*:** A Greek word for "conversion."

Millennialism: The belief associated with a thousand year period (millennium) in which Christ's reign is to flourish and prosper on earth.

Minister: A member of the clergy or one who serves in the Church.

Miracle: God intervening in the natural world in such a way that the end result appears to be contrary to or outside of the known laws of nature.

Modernism: The attempt to synthesize traditional religious beliefs with the theories of modern science.

Monasticism: The life pertaining to persons identified as monks living in religious or contemplative seclusion in places called monasteries.

Monism: The belief that there is but one fundamental reality that exists.

Monogenism: The theory that all humans originate ultimately from one man and one woman.

Monotheism: The belief that there is only one God.

Monophysitism: The Christological belief that denies the human nature of Jesus and teaches that he only possessed one nature and it was divine.

Moral theology: The application of Christian beliefs to the moral conduct of humans. Also called Christian ethics.

Mortal sin: A Roman Catholic reference to sin that is very serious or "deadly" that disrupts the good relationship that exists between God and a particular human being.

Nativity: Refers to the birth of Jesus at Bethlehem.

Natural law: The inherent and universal law written and engraved in every human being by God enabling a person to discern by reason between good and evil.

Nestorianism: A Christological belief named after Nestorius, bishop of Constantinople in the fifth century, who taught that there were two persons in Jesus Christ, a divine person and a human person, and Mary was the mother of the human Jesus only.

New Testament: The twenty-seven books that make up part of the Christian Bible dealing with the new covenant mediated by Jesus Christ.

Nicene Creed: A Christian statement of beliefs based primarily upon the decisions reached at the Council of Nicaea in 325 where Arianism was condemned.

Old Testament: That part of the Christian Bible containing those books describing the covenant God made with humans before the coming of Jesus Christ.

Omnipotence: Unlimited power, authority, or force. An attribute of God that describes him as all-powerful.

Omnipresence: Present everywhere. The attribute of God that describes him as everywhere present. *See* ubiquitous.

Omniscience: Totality of knowledge; knowing everything. An attribute of God alone that describes him as knowing everything that exists.

Ordination: The ceremony during which a person is invested with ministerial or priestly authority usually through a ritual of the "laying on of hands" by the ordaining person.

Original Sin: The sin of Adam and Eve inherited by all human beings.

Orthodoxy: Refers to "correct/right belief" in contrast to heresy. The term is also used with reference to the Eastern churches in communion with the Patriarch of Constantinople.

Panentheism: The belief that views God as being present in everything.

Parable: A simple story illustrating a moral or religious lesson.

Paraclete: Another name referring to the Holy Spirit who strengthens and guides the members of the church.

Paradise: A term commonly used to signify heaven, the abode of the angels, and the saints.

Parousia: The Greek word used in the New Testament to mean both "coming" and "presence" and in Christian eschatology refers to the second coming of Christ in his glory as king and judge.

Passover (Pesach): Jewish festival celebrated annually in the spring of the year commemorating the deliverance of the Israelites from Egyptian
slavery.

Pastor: A Christian minister in charge of a congregation.

Patriarch: One of the founders of the Israelites. A term also applied to certain leaders of the clergy in Eastern Orthodoxy and Roman Catholicism.

Pelagianism: The fifth century teachings of the British monk, Pelagius, and his followers who denied the doctrine of Original Sin and taught that humans can save themselves from sin without God's grace.

Pentecost: The annual Christian festival commemorating the descent of the Holy Spirit upon the church.

Pharisees: The political party of the synagogue in Judaism at the time of Jesus.

Pneumatology: That part of Christian theology dealing with the Holy Spirit.

Polygenism: The view that believes the origin of humans was derived from more than one man and one woman.

Polytheism: The belief in many gods.

Postmillennialism: The belief that the millennium will follow the *parousia* of Christ.

Predestination: The belief that before the creation of the world God determined/foreordained all that would come to pass in it.

Premillennialism: The belief that the millennium will precede the *parousia* of Christ.

Priest: A translation of the Greek *presbyteros* (also translated "elder") which is applied to a rank in some Christian clergy below a bishop but above a deacon who has the authority and power to give absolution and administer all sacraments except Orders. An intermediary between God and humans.

Prophet: A spokesperson for God in the Bible.

Providence: The belief that God is the moving force that guides his creation toward perfection.

Purgatory: A Roman Catholic belief in a state after death for those who have died in the grace and friendship of God but are not yet perfectly purified to enter heaven.

Rabbi: A teacher in Judaism. Also the ordained spiritual leader of a Jewish congregation.

Rapture: A premillennialist, eschatological description of a state of ecstasy experienced by the "saints" of God who will be preserved from the tribulations of the last days. Also called the "translation."

Rationalism: The theory that reason alone provides the only satisfactory justification for one's actions or beliefs.

Real Presence: A term used to refer to the belief in the actual, physical, true presence of Christ in the sacrament of the Eucharist.

Redemption: Restoring, reestablishing , saving, or getting back one's good relationship with God.

Regeneration: The term used to signify spiritual rebirth or renewal with a person's reception of grace.

Resurrection: A returning to life after one has died.

Revelation: The act of disclosing or making known that which formerly was unknown.

Righteousness: The state of being right and just. *See* justification.

Sacrament: A ritual instituted by Christ in which God's saving grace is distinctively operative.

Sacred: Holy, set apart, or dedicated for religious reasons.

Sacrifice: The acknowledgment of dependence upon and the offering of something to a deity in order to make oneself holy.

Sadducees: The political party of the Temple in Judaism at the time of Jesus.

Saint: A holy person who is in communion with God.

Salvation: The achieving of righteousness or being right and just with God. At God's initiative, the state of being saved from sin. *See* justification.

Sanctification: The process by which one becomes holy after having undergone Christian conversion.

Satan: A word from the Hebrew meaning "adversary" and is the proper name for the personification of evil in the world. *See* devil.

Schism: Refers to the voluntary act of separating oneself from the unity of the church.

Septuagint: A third century B.C. Greek translation of the Old Testament/Hebrew Scriptures.

***Shema*:** A Hebrew word meaning "hear" or "listen" and refers to the passage from Deuteronomy 6:4 that teaches strict monotheism.

Sheol: The name given in the Old Testament to the state of passivity and neutrality where the dead abide. The nether world; a kind of limbo.

Sin: An offense against God that is a conscious and deliberate violation of his will expressed in the revealed or natural law.

Soteriology: That part of Christian theology that is concerned with the study of salvation.

Soul: The spiritual entity described as the animating and vital principle in human beings.

Spiritual: Relating to supernatural and not natural, tangible, or material phenomena.

Supernatural: Not attributable to natural forces but to powers beyond the natural such as the divine.

Synagogue: From a Greek word meaning "assembly" referring to the place where Jews meet for religious study and prayer.

Synoptic Gospels: The accounts of the gospel found in the New Testament by Matthew, Mark and Luke that are very similar yet different from one another.

Talmud: The extended post-biblical commentary on the *Torah* in Judaism.

TaNaK: The technical term/acronym some scholars use to designate the Old Testament/Hebrew Scriptures which incorporates the *Torah* (Law), the *Nev(b)iim* (Prophets), and the *Kethuv(b)im* (Writings).

Teleology: The study of ends, final causes, goals, or purposes.

Tetragrammaton: A technical reference to the four consonantal Hebrew letters (*YHWH*) of God's proper name in the Old Testament usually called Yahweh. *See* Yahweh.

Thanatology: The study of death.

Theism: From the Greek word *theos* (God) and is the belief that God not only has created and sustains his creation in existence but is in contact with his creation through providence.

Theologian: A believer in a community of believers who reflects on his/her relationship with God and expresses it in clear and coherent language.

Theology: The study of the existence and nature of God and his relationship with his creation.

Theophany: The temporal and spatial manifestation of God in some tangible form.

***Torah*:** A Hebrew word for "law" but also refers to the first five books of the Old Testament/Hebrew Scriptures.

Transcendence: Existence above, beyond, and independent of the here and now.

Transfiguration: The divinity of God shining through the humanity of Jesus.

Translation: *See* rapture.

Trinity: The Christian belief that in the one God there are three distinct and equal persons traditionally called the Father, the Son, and the Holy Spirit/Ghost.

Ubiquitous: Being present everywhere at the same time. Omnipresent.

Ultimate Reality: Another name for God.

Vicarious: Performed or endured by one person substituting for another.

Virgin Birth: The miraculous conception and birth of Jesus by Mary without the intervention of a human male.

Vulgate: The Latin version of the Bible translated by St. Jerome in the fourth century that has been the most widely used Latin version in Western Christianity.

Wise Men: *See* Magi.

Yahweh: Proper name for God revealed to Moses in Ex. 3:14 and generally translated by some form of the verb "to be."

Zealots: The revolutionary party in Judaism at the time of Jesus.

Index

About the Author

JOHN C. MEYER is Associate Professor of Religious Studies in the Department of Philosophy and Religious Studies at Bradley University, Peoria, Illinois. He is a graduate of Loras College in Dubuque, Iowa with a B.A. degree; the University of Louvain, Belgium with M.A. and S.T.G. degrees; and the Catholic University of America in Washington, DC with a Ph.D. degree.

Before coming to Bradley University in 1969, Dr. Meyer had taught at Columbus High School in Waterloo, Iowa; St. Joseph's College of Emmitsburg, Maryland; the Catholic University of America; the University of Dubuque, Iowa; and Loras College.